To Shannon —

Thanks for a Great
Year !!

"Buns Up !!"
"Absolutly Absurd
Chances Are"

Two South Abbott
1976-7

PLANTS TO GROW IN THE HOME

PLANTS TO GROW
IN THE HOME

ANN BONAR

GALAHAD BOOKS

Contents

Published 1976 in the USA by
Galahad Books
A division of A & W Promotional Book Corp.
95 Madison Avenue, New York, NY 10016

© 1976 Octopus Books Limited

ISBN 0 88365 140 8

Produced by Mandarin Publishers Limited
22A Westlands Road, Quarry Bay, Hong Kong

Printed in Hong Kong

With special thanks to the House of Rochford
Selwyn Davidson and Bromage & Young
for many of the plants illustrated, and to
Casa Pupo for the containers

Introduction

Plants in the home nowadays can make a show as colourful and attractive as they once did in a well-cared-for Victorian hot-house. In the late nineteenth century greenhouses became available at popular prices, making it possible to grow all sorts of plants, in varying degrees of warmth. Some of the cooler-temperature plants, such as aspidistra, found their way into people's homes, and in this way the variety of plants grown indoors increased steadily in number.

It was not until the Second World War, however, when fuel became so short, that people realized how many plants would accept quite low winter temperatures, 10° or 7°C (50° or 45°F), without damage. Since then, more and more homes have acquired central heating, of one kind or another, during the winter. On top of all this, and perhaps because of it, new plants for the home have been sought out by nurserymen, with much breeding and selection of good hybrids and strains.

Knowledge of how to care for indoor plants has been gained through experience, particularly in the last twenty years, and from the plants described and illustrated in this book you will see that there is today a plant for every room in the house which is ornamental either in colour or form, or both. Growing a strong healthy plant is very satisfying in itself, even to the extent of being addictive—be warned that the gift of one small Bead Plant may lead eventually to the absolute necessity of building a garden room, no less, on to the house.

Whether you are given indoor plants or are going to choose your own, instead of putting them in the nearest convenient place, think first whether that position is going to suit them. To give an extreme example, if you put a cactus in a dark corner of the hall, it will languish miserably and finally die, but if you put it on a windowsill where it gets as much sun as possible, it will grow, and flower, and produce young. A shade-loving plant such as ivy put in too warm and light a place will stop growing, its leaves will brown and wither, and it will probably become infested with pests. When you buy indoor plants from a reputable supplier they should have brief details giving advice on position and care, and you will find that putting plants in a position which supplies a suitable environment is half the battle.

At the same time, you will want to show off your plants to the best advantage, whether they are positioned singly or in groups. Be careful when you group plants together that they have the same requirements of light, temperature, humidity, and so on. You can grow them in pots placed in a trough, or planted direct into it; you can plant several into a large bowl; you can make miniature gardens with the smaller plants; you can even make a set piece in a corner of the room, a miniature forest with climbers and orchids.

You can use climbing plants as dividers, or to frame picture windows or mirrors; you can set up a desert scene, a water garden or a bromeliad jungle. You can grow plants in a plant window, which is a trough the length of a floor-to-ceiling window, placed on the floor. Or you can have vertical plant groups, by growing them in a tower pot, one of the newest ideas, and really very effective; the plants seem to like it, too.

As well as choosing the right position, starting with good healthy plants is very important. When you buy a plant, make sure that it isn't wilting, that its leaves are not damaged, turning yellow, or brown, or about to fall off, and that its roots are not coming out of the bottom of the pot. Choose a flowering plant that is mostly in bud, with only a few flowers out, and have a particularly good look to make sure there are no pests like greenfly, scale or mealy bug on the leaves or stems. Plants are not cheap nowadays, and you would not buy a damaged product, so why buy an ailing plant?

When you are bringing it home, the nursery or shop should have wrapped it up well but, if not, try to provide some cover for the whole plant to protect it against cold and draughts. The changes in environment since it left its home nursery will have been considerable, and it is important to minimize these as much as possible, and to fuss over it a bit for the first few days while it settles down.

It may need watering at once; if the pot feels light and the compost is dry on the surface, try immersing the whole container in tepid water. If air bubbles come up through the water, the plant has been allowed to get very dry, and it is best left in the water until no more air bubbles appear. Then it can be taken out, the surplus water allowed to drain through the drainage holes, and put in its permanent position, on an ordinary saucer or pot saucer to prevent the damp damaging your furniture.

To water the plant in the normal way, fill the space between the soil surface and the pot rim, about 1–2.5 cm ($\frac{1}{2}$–1 in) in depth, fairly quickly with water, repeat and then let it drain. Watering should be done only when the surface is dry—it may be necessary daily, or every few days, or only occasionally, depending on the type of plant, its size, and the temperature. It should never be done by rote, regularly every Saturday at 11 o'clock.

The plant must never be allowed to wilt. If the lower leaves begin to turn yellow, it often means that you are overwatering, and the plant must be left severely alone until it has dried out somewhat. With experience, you will find that the plants themselves will tell you when they need water. Try to use rainwater, at room temperature, or tap water which has been allowed to stand. With some plants, it is safer to water them from below, by standing them in a shallow dish of water, and letting it soak up through the compost.

Almost as important as the supply of water is the supply of humidity. Practically every plant, except cacti and other succulents, some bromeliads and one or two miscellaneous cast-iron plants, need a moist atmosphere. Without it, leaf tips and edges turn brown, brown spots appear in the centre of the leaves, flowers and buds drop off, and finally the leaves will drop. Humidity is vital for a plant's health. When the temperature rises over 21°C (70°F) the atmosphere will need a great deal of extra moisture—the humidity should be about 50–60%.

A large shallow dish, containing water and shingle for the plant to stand on out of the wet, is a good way of supplying humidity. Another method is to stand the container on an upturned bowl in another larger bowl containing water—this is probably better for those plants which need plenty of humidity. Better still, and better for you too, especially with central heating, is to use humidifiers. There are kinds which can be hung on radiators, or electric models which are completely quiet and can be adjusted to release varying amounts of moisture.

Misting the plants every day is very acceptable to them. Special

An attractive grouping, all excellent indoor plants: African violet, Chlorophytum comosum Vittatum, Ficus pumila, Zebrina pendula, Chamaedorea elegans

sprayers can be bought from garden shops which deliver the water (tepid or at room temperature) in a fine mist-like stream. Ordinary overhead spraying is good for the larger plants, and you should also wipe the leaves with a clean, moist sponge or soft cloth. This gets rid of dust and dirt at the same time and, incidentally, often enables you to spot a pest or disease before it has had time to do any real damage.

Plants drink a lot of their food and they need quantities of mineral elements which are mostly absorbed from the compost or potting mix. Three very important minerals are nitrogen, phosphorus and potassium, and proprietary plant foods contain varying percentages of these; the amounts present are marked on the product packet under what is called the analysis, for example, N 5%, P_2O_5 6%, K_2O 7%. In this particular analysis the plant foods are present in balanced and average quantities. However, some fertilizers have a good deal more nitrogen (N), which helps leaf and shoot growth, and others have a lot of potassium (K), important for flowering and fruiting. So you should choose a fertilizer depending on whether you have plants which are grown mainly for the leaves or flowers.

The most convenient way to feed plants in pots is with a liquid fertilizer, usually given once a week during the growing period. Most composts or mixes contain some plant food, so there is no need to start feeding for several weeks or even months after potting.

The smaller, softer, quickly growing plants such as Busy Lizzie and the Aluminium Plant (*Pilea cadierei*) can be made more bushy by 'pinching'. This means nipping out the tip of a shoot when the plant is growing well, removing the stem with the first pair, and sometimes the second pair, of leaves from the tip, and making the cut or break just above the next lowest pair, so that no stub is left on the plant. New shoots will then grow lower down from between the stem and the point where a leaf joins the stem, but the tip of the shoot will not grow any more. 'Pinching' can be done two or three times at about monthly intervals in spring and early summer.

'Resting' plants is very important; it is usually needed after flowering, though some plants have a slightly different life cycle and go on growing after this for a while. To rest a plant, gradually give it less water, and put it in a lower temperature than when it is growing. Sometimes the shoots need to be cut right back. The plant becomes almost dormant and may remain like that for several months; its rest period may be in summer or winter, depending on the flowering time which will vary according to which part of the world it comes from.

The ideal compost or potting mix for your indoor plants needs to be of such a texture that it will contain air and water, but not to the extent that it gets waterlogged. There are various ready-made-up brands available and references throughout the text of this book are based on the John Innes composts for seed growing and potting.

The John Innes seed compost contains 2 parts loam, 1 part peat and 1 part coarse sand (parts by volume) together with 43 grams ($1\frac{1}{2}$ ounces) superphosphate and 21 grams ($\frac{3}{4}$ ounce) chalk per bushel of the mixture. John Innes Potting Compost No. 1 consists of 7 parts loam, 3 parts peat and 2 parts sand, plus 112 grams (4 ounces) base fertilizer and 21 grams ($\frac{3}{4}$ ounce) chalk per bushel. The base fertilizer is made up of 2 parts hoof and horn (13% N), 2 parts superphosphate (18% P_2O_5) and 1 part sulphate of potash (48% K_2O) (parts by weight); this can also be bought ready made-up and added if you are making your own compost. To be true John Innes compost, the loam should be sterilized, but if not you can still get good results for indoor plants. The chalk should be left out of the mix for plants which prefer acid soil conditions. John Innes Potting Compost No. 2 and No. 3 contain twice as much and three times as much, respectively, of chalk and fertilizer. John Innes No. 2 is used for plants in 12.5–20-cm (5–8-in) pots; John Innes No. 3 is for anything larger.

The modern so-called soilless composts contain, usually, 75% peat and 25% sand if for potting use and can be bought made up, some with and some without nutrient added. Seed mixes consist of 50% each of fine sand and peat, to which fertilizer should be added.

The time to repot most plants is in spring, when growth is just starting again, but in general repotting after the plant's resting period is a good rule to follow. Only repot when the roots have filled the soil ball, and give the plant a drink some hours before you repot. In most cases use a size larger pot, but remember that some plants flower better if potbound.

Put broken pieces of clay pot, concave side up, at the bottom of new clay pots (but not plastic ones) for drainage, and add a little compost or potting mix. Put your left hand over the surface of the old pot, turn the plant and pot upside down and, holding the pot in your right hand, tap the rim against your working surface. The soil ball should then fall out intact into your left hand. Put the plant centrally into the new pot so that it is at the same level as before and fill in compost or potting mix down the sides. Firm the top with your fingers until it is level with the top of the soil ball. Give one quick watering, and leave the plant to drain.

Increasing indoor plants is done, in most cases, by taking cuttings. These are the top 7.5 cm (3 in) or so of a new shoot—you can use the tips taken from pinching out—and they should be pushed straight into a compost or potting mix, up against the side of the pot. Two, three or four cuttings can go in one pot. Remove the lowest leaf or pair of leaves, and cut the stem off cleanly just below the point where these leaves were attached. If you are using loam-based compost or potting mix and you have inserted your cuttings correctly, a gentle pull on a leaf will not shift them, but soilless composts or mixes should not be firmed down hard. Place a blown-up, clear plastic bag over the pot, secure it with an elastic band round the pot rim, and leave the cuttings in a warm shaded place to root. Proprietary hormone powders and solutions are sometimes needed with obstinate cuttings.

You may find that, in spite of all your care, your plants are not thriving as they should. Usually this means that either what is your idea of a little water is the plant's idea of too much, or your views on the amount of warmth required do not coincide. In practically every case of poor plant growth, the remedy is to alter your care and management of it, to give less or more water, less or more humidity, change the temperature or the light, repot, and so on. Weak plants, or plants which are having to contend with the wrong environment, are the ones which will be infected by insect pests. Healthy plants are usually not attacked.

The main pests are greenfly, mostly on the tips of shoots and on young leaves; red spider mites, minute red pests on the undersurface of leaves, spinning webs and producing yellowish speckling; scale insects, round or oval slightly raised brown spots on leaf undersurfaces near the veins, and on stems and bark; mealy bugs, with a white fluffy coating, on leaves and stems; and root bugs, like greenfly, but with a white wool-like substance to protect them, feeding on roots.

All these suck the sap from plants, weaken them seriously and stunt the new growth. Treat with resmethrin and repeat the spray once or twice more at about weekly intervals. Scale insects and mealy bugs should be scraped off first, as completely as possible, with the back of a knife.

Brown edges and tips of leaves usually mean a dry atmosphere; brown spots indicate too low or too high a temperature; yellowing leaves eventually falling from evergreen plants mean too much water, or draughts; dropping buds and flowers occur in dry atmospheres, gas, draughts, sudden changes of temperature, or if the plant is moved; leaves wilting, too much or too little water; variegated leaves becoming plain green, not enough light; azaleas with thickened grey leaves (a fungus infection), cut off affected leaves and flowers; holes in leaf edges, slugs; grey mould on leaves or rotting of crowns or tubers, cold and/or too much water.

To help you in your choice of plants to grow indoors, the name of each plant described is marked with a symbol:* means the plant is easy to grow;** means a plant that requires more care; *** means a rather difficult and temperamental plant.

The beautiful hibiscus hybrid Moonlight

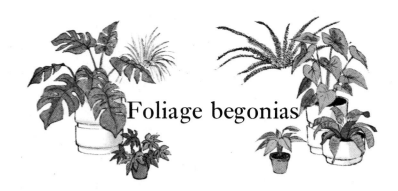

Foliage begonias

Rex ✳✳ , *masoniana* (Iron Cross) ✳✳ , *maculata* ✳ , *metallica* ✳

The Rex begonias are extremely attractive plants with magnificent leaves in shades of deep or light red with grey or silvery markings, or with deep red centres and wide green edges, spotted and lined with white, crimson or grey. The picture gives an idea of the variety of striking patterns the leaves can have, and a group of these begonias will be as colourful as any flowering plant.

The begonias come from all over the world, but they are mainly found in eastern Asia and Central America, where the climate is moist and warm. Many grow in forests. They were named after Michel Begon, a patron of botany who lived during the nineteenth century; *B. rex* was introduced in 1858.

The Rex begonias are part of the rhizomatous-rooted (creeping underground stems) group and do not grow to more than about 300 mm (1 ft) tall, with about the same spread. The leaves become quite large, from about 20–30 cm (8–12 in) long and at least 15 cm (6 in) wide. If they flower, the colour will be pink, but it is better to remove flowering stems so that the plant produces more leaves.

As indoor plants, Rex begonias will grow best in a shady place, away from the sun which scorches them brown and dries them up very quickly. They also like a humid atmosphere, and will not do well in central heating unless you are very conscientious about providing moist air and misting them with water two or three times a day. You can give them humidity by standing the container on gravel or on an upturned saucer in a wide shallow dish kept filled with water, so that it evaporates up round the leaves constantly. Misting the leaves with water at least once a day is also appreciated, but actual spraying which leaves drops of water on the foliage will result in brown spots. As you might imagine, knowing the kind of place in which they grow naturally, Rex begonias like to be warm, ideally 16–21°C (60–70°F). If the temperature drops lower than this in the winter, they will not be harmed, provided the compost is kept slightly on the dry side, but anything below 10°C (50°F) will kill. In summer, the temperature can go up to 21–25°C (70–80°F), but always in the shade. Begonias do not like draughts and the one thing they are extremely allergic to is gas, so keep them well away from it.

Watering will depend on the season. In spring and summer the plants grow quite fast and, being mainly leaf, will lose a lot of water, so they will need watering perhaps twice a week, more or less depending on the size of the plant, the temperature and the type of compost. Fill the space at the top of the pot with water (at room temperature) in the usual way, let it soak right through and drain off any surplus. Then leave the begonia severely alone until the compost surface lightens in colour, and it looks and feels dry. In winter once a week or less is all the watering that is likely to be needed, but do tailor it to the amount the plant shows it needs by its appearance.

If you have potted the plant on (in spring, I hope), it will not need feeding until mid-summer, perhaps not even then. Use a liquid feed which the analysis on the container shows to have more N (nitrogen) than anything else, as this is the nutrient needed for good leafy growth. Stop feeding in autumn, or whenever the plant ceases to produce new leaves, indicating that it wants a rest.

Begonias need a compost containing a good deal of humus, such as peat or leafmould. Sometimes a newly bought plant is more than ready for a larger pot and new compost.

If you want more plants, for yourself or to give to friends, leaf begonias can be increased by using the leaves themselves. Cut off a leaf, make cuts here and there across the main veins, and put the leaf on the surface of moist sand in a shallow pot. Keep the leaf in contact with the sand by weighing it down with stones, and cover the container with glass. In a warm (21°C, 70°F) shady place, roots and plantlets will grow from the cuts, but if the sand or the atmosphere is too damp the leaf will rot before it can root.

The Rex begonias are not the only good leafy begonias there are to grow. The one that used to be called 'Iron Cross', and is now *B. masoniana*, has a lightish green leaf, with a very obvious dark wine-red marking extending out from the centre, like a cross. The surface of the leaf itself is unusual; it is almost corrugated, with pimples on the top of the corrugations.

The leaves of *B. maculata* are very handsomely spotted in silvery white on dark green with an underneath of red; they are long and narrow, and there is a bonus of pink flowers in summer. It likes slightly lower temperatures than *B. rex* and can grow up to 90 cm (3 ft) tall; its roots are fibrous. *B. metallica* is in the same root group, but has shining green wrinkled leaves with black veins on the upper side which give it its metallic look. It also produces pale pink flowers in summer and autumn. It grows to 1.2 m (4 ft), but you can cut it back hard in spring, repotting it at the same time. You can use the shoot tips, 10 cm (4 in) long, for making new cuttings.

The leaves of the Begonia rex hybrids are strikingly beautiful in their colouring

Flowering begonias

Double-flowered ** , *semperflorens* * , Gloire de Lorraine * , *haageana* *

The double-flowered tuberous begonias so widely grown are exotic plants from South America. Although a greenhouse is needed to grow them to perfection, they will be quite alright in the house, where they will probably grow a little taller. You can buy named varieties, such as Tahiti (orange), Sugar Candy (pink), Buttermilk (golden cream) or Corona (yellow with frilly red edges), or unnamed seedlings, which are less expensive but just as beautiful.

Buy or send for the tubers in early spring, and put them into shallow containers in a light place, root side downwards, just covering them with moist peat. The top of the round tuber will be flattish, slightly hollow even, with perhaps some fragments of last year's stem on it, the underneath rounded. In about four weeks, new shoots should appear from the top of the tuber, and by then roots will have started to grow into the peat. Sprouting will be quicker if the container is covered with glass; remember not to let the peat become dry. Take off the glass when growth starts and pot the tubers when the shoots are about 10 cm (4 in) tall, singly into a 10-cm (4-in) pot containing John Innes Potting Compost No. 1 (see page 8). When the roots have reached the sides of the pot, move the plant again into a 15–18-cm (6–7-in) pot of John Innes Potting Compost No. 2 (see page 8).

When the plants begin to produce flower buds, you will find that the centre flower only—the male—is double, and the females on either side are single. If you remove the female flowers with their stalks, this will help the male flowers to grow bigger.

The begonias need a temperature of 16–20°C (60–70°F) to start sprouting, and then need to be kept at about 16°C (60°F) or more for the season. They will do well in sun to start with, but as the light becomes stronger they should be moved to a window-sill out of the direct sunlight. Keep the atmosphere moist, to prevent bud drop.

Water very carefully: at first keep the compost just moist, but as the plant comes into full growth and flowering give it much more water. Once the buds appear, you will find that slightly too much or too little water will result in bud drop, so be particularly careful at this stage. As flowering ends, gradually give them less water until the leaves have dropped.

Feed these plants occasionally, every two or three weeks, with a liquid feed containing a high potash content, from the time the flower buds appear. When the plant has obviously reached its dormant period, after the leaves have fallen, either twist the stems gently off or let them drop off naturally. Store the tuber either in the pot without watering, or in dry peat or sand, in a frostproof place until February.

The single-flowered fibrous-rooted begonias produce their small flowers in clusters, sometimes drooping; the effect is graceful and delicate, and you may find them more attractive than the heavier double flowers. The *semperflorens* begonias flower all through the summer, in small clumps about 23 cm (9 in) tall and as much across. They will be covered in flowers, rose-pink, pale pink, pink and white, or white with bright yellow centres, and with very dark wine red or light green leaves. The white-flowered variety with dark red leaves is outstanding.

Cultivation of *semperflorens* is easy: give them good light, normal summer temperatures, a compost rich in humus, some humidity and plenty of water. If you keep the plants warm, they will continue flowering into or all through the winter, but it is better to give them a rest for three months or so, lowering the temperature and watering very little. Cut them back in the spring and repot, or give liquid feed regularly. If they drop their leaves or buds, you must alter your care, giving less or more water, a different temperature, a more humid atmosphere, or a different position away from a draught or bright light.

The Gloire de Lorraine type of begonias can be bought in flower near Christmas and will continue flowering throughout the winter. The colours are the same as the *semperflorens* types, but there are fewer varieties. Give them the same conditions as the summer-flowering begonias, with a temperature of about 13°C (55°F). When flowering has finished, cut the plant back to a few inches, and dry off until late spring, then repot in a rich humus compost and start watering. Nip out the tips of the shoots at intervals to make the plant bushier and delay flowering until the winter. These tips can be used for cuttings. Bud drop will occur if the plant is moved at all, or watered with cold water; it should always be slightly warm.

White powdery spots and patches on the leaves, stems and sometimes flowers of any of these begonias are due to the fungus disease mildew. Their appearance is usually a sign that you are not growing the plants the right way, and you will therefore need to change your treatment. Meanwhile the affected parts should be cut off and the plant sprayed with benomyl or dinocap, or dusted with sulphur.

Begonia haageana is named after Herr Haage, a German seedsman of the nineteenth century. It is easy to grow but needs plenty of space, as it will reach 60 cm (2 ft) even if it is stopped fairly often. It has large hairy red leaves and foot-wide flower clusters which are rose-pink in summer. Give it plenty of light (but not strong sunlight) and water in summer, and a winter temperature not lower than 7°C (45°F).

See also 'Summer-flowering Plants'.

Begonia semperflorens is a fibrous-rooted species which blooms for many months of the year

Trailing plants

Hedera species (ivy)＊, *Tradescantia fluminensis* Variegata (Wandering Jew)＊, *Zebrina pendula*＊, *Gynura* Sarmentosa (Purple Passion Vine)＊＊, *Campanula isophylla* (Italian Bellflower)＊

This is a group of plants, mostly grown for their leaves, which are virtually foolproof and will continue to grow in spite of any amount of neglect. Unfortunately they often are neglected, with the result that the colours of the leaves become faded, and the growth is straggly and weak. The ivies and the campanula can, of course, be grown vertically.

Ivy likes to be grown in quite cool rooms, with a moist atmosphere. If the conditions are too warm and dry, the leaves go brown at the edges, dry up and fall off, and the plant will get infested with red spider mite and blackfly. If grown in a poor light, the variegated ivies gradually change to plain green. Practically all the ivies are hardy, so they are good plants to grow if you do not have much extra heat available in winter. They will not do well in central heating.

The plain green-leaved *Hedera helix* is the common ivy; smaller-leaved kinds are *sagittaefolia* (arrow-shaped), which has smaller leaves with the central lobe very long, Glacier, with creamy edges to a three-lobed grey-green leaf, and Goldheart, bright, deep yellow centres to dark green leaves. A good large-leaved ivy is the Canary Island species which used to be called Gloire de Marengo and is now rather prosaically Variegata; the leaf edges are broadly and irregularly creamy, and the rest of the leaf green and grey-green. The stems are red. There are many more ivies, but these will give you a start.

Keep the plants cool, in summer particularly, and spray overhead daily. They like a good light, with feed and plenty of water in summer. Shoot tips broken off and stuck in compost at almost any time will root.

Tradescantia and zebrina are commonly regarded as being rather similar plants to look at, but in fact they are quite different. However, they can be grown in the same way. Tradescantia was named after John Tradescant, a plant collector and gardener to Charles I; zebrina was named after the zebra, because of the stripes on the leaves.

Tradescantia is best grown in the variegated form with light green and white- or yellow-striped leaves, which will turn pink at the edges if you keep the plant slightly on the dry side; the colouring is most marked when it is kept in a well-lit place. Any plain green shoots which appear should be removed at once. The species called *albiflora* Albovittata is like *fluminensis*, but altogether larger and fleshier, and stiffer in habit of growth.

Water freely in summer, and put it in a cool place, both summer and winter. Misting frequently will prevent browning. John Innes Potting Compost No. 1 (see page 8) is the best compost, with only occasional liquid feeding in summer. The tips of shoots will root quickly in spring or summer in either compost or plain water.

The same treatment will suit zebrina, which grows rather more upright while young, but in time will hang over the edge of the container. It is a larger, fleshier and much more colourful plant than tradescantia; the leaves are silvery green, centred with a purple-green stripe and purplish underneath, and the flowers are purple. It can be made to grow bushily for a time, by pinching out the tops of the shoots.

You may have seen a plant in the florist's window with beautiful purple-furry leaves and stems and wondered what it was; *Gynura* Sarmentosa is its botanical name—the Purple Passion Vine is its common name. It comes from India and has small orange flowers in clusters in summer, but its leaves are the reason for its popularity.

Young plants are the best-coloured—the older ones become rather green. Tip cuttings taken in spring will root if kept very warm, about 24°C (75°F), in a plastic bag.

Gynura needs humidity at all times, with frequent misting, and the use of the shallow dish method (see page 6). Put it in a well-lit place and give it plenty of water in summer. Liquid feeding will maintain new growth, and good drainage is important; you should add extra sand to the compost and broken pieces of pot to the container.

The Italian Bellflower is a delicate-looking plant, with masses of fragile pale blue or white bells about 2.5 cm (1 in) wide from July, sometimes earlier, until autumn. The white-flowered variety is *Campanula isophylla* Alba. It is very pretty hanging down over the sides of the container, and easily grown—it can be planted outdoors in mild gardens, so does not need much heat in winter. Give it moderate humidity and gentle sunlight.

Growth starts again in spring, and as the new shoots appear you can take cuttings from them, rooting them in compost or plain water, and potting them into small 5-cm (2-in) pots to start with. On the parent plant, the shoots will gradually lengthen till they hang over the edge of the pot, and plenty of water and feeding are essential for good flowering. Remove the flowers as soon as they are dead, as this campanula is inclined to exhaust itself. When flowering has finished for the season, it will die down and should be cut back hard to leave only an inch or so of stem, drying it off almost completely at the same time. Keep it cool and barely moist through the winter, then start to water normally in early spring. Repot in the third season in fresh John Innes Potting Compost No. 1 (see page 8).

See also 'The Fig Family'.

Trailing plants look their best in a hanging basket: the green ivy Hedera helix Chicago and the variegated Eva, with Tradescantia albiflora below

Leafy climbing plants

Cissus antarctica (Kangaroo Vine)∗ , *Philodendron scandens*
(*P. cordatum, P. oxycardium*) (Sweetheart Vine)∗ ,
Cissus rhombifolia (Grape Ivy)∗

If you are looking for easy-care foliage plants for the house, these
plants are nearly indestructible and grow reasonably quickly.
They will provide cover or division for open plan rooms, frames
for windows, mirrors and pictures, and cover for awkward spaces
and bare corners.

A favourite climbing plant is cissus, which comes from a Greek
word meaning ivy. There are various cissus species, most of
which are climbers, with tendrils which will coil round supports
as soon as they are provided. The most commonly grown is *C.
antarctica*, the Kangaroo Vine, named for its Australian ancestry, not because it grows in leaps and bounds; actually it grows
quite steadily. The leaves are shiny green, toothed at the edges
and about 10 cm (4 in) long. It will grow 60 cm (2 ft) or more in a
season to a final height of about 2.4 m (8 ft). Instead of training it
vertically, try growing it on cane circles or triangles, or up a fan-
shaped support.

The Kangaroo Vine, like many leafy climbers, does not like
bright sunlight but thrives in a good general light or shade.
Humidity is essential, either in the atmosphere or in the form of
daily overhead spraying, and the leaves are all the better for an
occasional sponging. Putting it out in summer showers will do it
a power of good. The temperature in winter can drop as low as
4°C (40°F), but keep the plant slightly on the dry side and, in any
case, water only very moderately in winter while it is resting. It
will need fairly generous watering in summer, as it is a vigorous
grower.

Cissus discolor is an attractive species, with leaves in a startling
mixture of colours, but, unlike the other species, it is very difficult to grow.

The John Innes composts (see page 8) cannot be improved
upon, and feeding from midsummer onwards with a nitrogenous
liquid fertilizer will keep the leaves a good glossy green. Most
varieties of cissus will stand gas in the atmosphere (an exception
is *C. sicyoides*). The plants also survive draughts and sudden
drops in temperature. In bright sunlight the leaves will turn pale
brown or yellowish green, and too much warmth will result in
leaf drop.

In late February, just before growth starts again, you can cut
the plant back to keep it within a reasonable space. Increase from
10-cm (4-in)-long tip cuttings, which will root in compost or
just water on its own.

The philodendrons also make good indoor plants—some are
climbing, others not, but they all have attractive and unusually
shaped leaves. The Sweetheart Vine, *P. scandens* (*P. cordatum,
P. oxycardium*), twines its way enthusiastically up its supporting
and possibly reluctant host. In the wild the host would be a tree,
and this explains the plant's name which comes from two Greek
words, *phileo*, to love, and *dendron*, a tree. The tropical forests of
the West Indies and Panama are its natural home, but it is surprisingly easy to grow indoors and is adaptable to many
conditions.

The leaves have a heart-shaped base, hence the common name,
and taper off to a point, with an overall length when full-grown
of 30 cm (12 in). Both leaves and stems are rather thick and
fleshy, which means that plenty of water is needed in summer.
Daily overhead spraying or a moderately humid atmosphere is
necessary, and the temperature in winter should not be lower
than 7°C (45°F), higher if possible. They also like shade. Plant
philodendrons in John Innes composts (see page 8) and feed
from mid-summer until autumn with a nitrogen-high liquid
fertilizer. If you want a slightly more bushy plant, nip out the
growing tips occasionally or cut the whole plant back in late
February.

The Sweetheart Vine is a member of a family of plants which
produce aerial roots from the leaf joints on the stems. If you
train the plant up a length of damp cork bark or sphagnum-
moss-covered cane, these roots will attach themselves to the bark
or moss and improve the plant's vigour.

You can increase from stem cuttings, but they will need a temperature of 24°C (75°F) and a very moist atmosphere in order
to root.

Another popular climbing plant is the Grape Ivy, *Cissus
rhombifolia*, which in very favourable conditions produces very
small grape-shaped berries. It will grow into a large plant in
three seasons, but will be rather sprawling and bushy unless you
provide it with plenty of canes to which it can attach its tendrils.
An awkward dark corner of a room can be cheered up by putting
a piece of trellis against the wall and training the shoots up it, but
if repotting is needed, do this first—it will be difficult afterwards.

The leaves are toothed and consist of three diamond-shaped
glossy leaflets; if you put the plant in bright sunlight they will
turn yellow and the plant will stop growing. It much prefers a
shady place, on the cool side. In summer it can stand outdoors,
out of the sun, and will enjoy the freshening effect of summer
showers. Water plentifully in summer, much less in winter, and
keep the temperature in winter not lower than 7°C (45°F), higher
if possible. A dry atmosphere will affect the leaves, making the
edges turn brown until finally they curl up and fall off, so spray
the plant regularly and keep the atmosphere moist.

Use John Innes composts (see page 8), and feed with a
nitrogen-high liquid fertilizer from mid-summer to winter. Topdress in spring if repotting is difficult, and do any cutting back
that is necessary in late February. You can increase from the cuttings, but they will need bottom heat to root, and are therefore
not as obliging.

See also 'The Fig Family'.

*The Grape Ivy, Cissus rhombifolia, a member of the same family as the
grape, is a vigorous climber*

Flowering climbing plants

Dipladenia sanderi✻✻, *Hoya carnosa* (Wax-flower)✻✻, *Passiflora caerulea* (Passion-flower)✻

The secret of getting flowering climbing plants to actually flower in the home is to give them as much light as possible (with the exception of the midday sun). The ordinary climbers which are grown because they have attractive leaves are used to growing in shade; those that flower in their native home have managed at some time to reach the light, which seems to encourage the change from leafy growth to flowery.

Dipladenia twines compactly round its supports, and has pretty rose-pink, trumpet-shaped flowers, rather like convolvulus. June to late August or September is its main blooming time, but flowers are produced occasionally in spring and autumn as well. The evergreen leaves are dark green and glossy.

Dipladenia comes from Brazil, and you will need to keep the temperature up in winter, and very humid, otherwise it will die. At least 13°C (55°F) is needed, and a constantly moist atmosphere. If you have a well-lit and centrally heated bathroom, you will probably find this is the best place. In summer, daily misting and frequent watering are essential, but let it rest in winter by giving hardly any water until February, just enough to keep the compost moist, then gradually increase it.

Any cutting back is done in October, when flowering has finished; just take off the shoots which have flowered. A very peaty compost is best, and you will need to feed from May till autumn, once a week. Increasing the plant is not easy, as the cuttings need a temperature of 27°C (80°F) in late winter, but if you do try it, use a mixture of sand and peat.

The Wax-flower, *Hoya carnosa*, is named after Thomas Hoy, who was one of the Duke of Northumberland's gardeners at Syon House, Brentford, in the late 1700s. As a native of Queensland, Australia, it is particularly happy in sun, which needs to be very hot and bright before a hoya will complain. Its pink star-shaped flowers, looking as if they are made of wax, grow stiffly in clusters on long twining stems to about 3.5 m (12 ft) long. The plant will need a good deal of space eventually, but this can be got over by training it round circles of cane, which looks very attractive. It flowers from late May through to autumn.

The evergreen leaves are rather thick and can store moisture, but nevertheless it needs careful watering; give plenty when the plant is growing and in full flower, but much less from the time the flower buds appear until they open. The same applies to liquid feeding—give a little during the growing season, but stop altogether when the flower buds show, otherwise they will drop without opening. They will also drop if the pot is moved.

Like the dipladenia, hoya prefers a peaty compost. If the leaves begin to turn pale green, then yellow, suspect overwatering, a limey compost, hard water or too much hot sun, and alter your care accordingly.

In winter the temperature can drop to 7°C (45°F), provided much less water is given. If the plant needs cutting back, do it in February.

When the flowers have finished, you can take them off, but leave the flower stalk behind because new flowers will be produced from its base the following year, even sometimes in the same year. Beware mealy bug, which is partial to hoya. Increase by layering shoots in spring or summer.

Of all the fascinating flowers, the passion flower, *Passiflora caerulea*, is probably one of the most interesting. It always attracts attention, and although the flowers only last a day, there are so many that there are always some in full bloom from May until autumn.

The name was given to it because the floral parts seemed to represent the Passion of Christ; the filaments (the blue, white and purple tendrils) are the crown of thorns, the stigmas (at the top of the central column) the three nails, the stamens below them the five wounds. The ten sepals and petals are the apostles (excepting Judas and Peter). The plant comes from Central and South America, and was discovered at the time when the Aztecs were being 'converted' by the Spaniards to Roman Catholicism.

There are many highly ornamental species of passiflora, some with scarlet flowers, but *P. caerulea* is the one which takes most kindly to growing indoors, and will in fact grow outdoors against a wall in mild gardens. Indoors, it is a good fast-growing plant, climbing by tendrils. The blue, white, purple and greenish flowers with bright yellow-orange stamens are about 10 cm (4 in) wide.

Although a vigorous grower, it will not be harmed by being confined to a large pot or tub, and will in fact flower better with this restriction to its rather fleshy, tuberous roots. It needs plenty of water in summer and a sunny position, otherwise the buds will not open.

In winter the temperature can drop to 7°C (45°F), or a little lower, provided watering is considerably lessened. The leaves will drop, and to encourage good flowering in the coming season, you should cut out the weak shoots and cut back the strong ones by about one-third in late February.

Use John Innes Potting Compost No. 1 or 2 (see page 8), depending on the size of the plant; it should be well-drained but not rich, otherwise the plant will produce leaf rather than flower. For the same reason, only feed occasionally. Spray the plant frequently overhead, to keep red spider mite at bay, and watch for greenfly which may infect it with virus. Do not grow passiflora in rooms where there are gas or open fires. Tip cuttings will root in water in spring.

The plants will sometimes produce orange egg-shaped fruits; these are edible, though rather insipid. The flavour is improved by mixing sherry or madeira with the flesh.

See also 'Plants to Grow from Seed'.

Passiflora caerulea, the Blue Passion Flower, also bears edible orange fruits

Green foliage plants I

Aspidistra elatior∗ , *Peperomia caperata*∗∗ , *P. marmorata*∗∗ ,
P. magnoliaefolia∗∗ , *Pilea involucrata*∗ , *P. microphylla*∗

It is difficult to believe that the aspidistra is a member of the same plant family as the lilies, and even more so if you are ever fortunate enough to own a plant which blooms. The dark purple flowers grow straight out of the soil and lie close against it, looking like small mushrooms until the top rolls back to form half a dozen or so petals. They appear in winter.

The aspidistra was introduced to England in 1822, and became very popular with the Victorians; it seems to be coming back into favour now, with the fashion for Victoriana. It can live to a very great age—one specimen is recorded as being over 60 years old—and is among the easiest and most amenable of indoor plants.

The dark green, shining leaves are undoubtedly handsome, growing from the soil without a central stem and arching over. The average leaf length is about 30 cm (1 ft), so a fully grown plant in its pot will be about 60 cm (2 ft). *A.e.* Variegata has longitudinal cream stripes.

Aspidistras are said to be able to withstand long periods without water, very little light, gas, tea, coffee and beer, no food, and considerable cold. This is an unnecessarily hard life, though; if you treat your plant like a plant, you will get a marvellous specimen which will flower, and which can be divided for propagation.

The aspidistra originally comes from China and the Himalayas; shade and a winter temperature of not less than 7°C (45°F) suit it best, with some humidity. The variegated kind needs more light to retain its markings. This is a plant whose leaves thrive on being cleaned by sponging every two or three weeks or the occasional bath in a summer shower. During summer a temperature on the cool side is preferred, and it can be put out of doors in the shade. Watering should be moderate, even less in winter. John Innes potting composts (see page 8) can be used, but it is not a greedy feeder so constant repotting will not be necessary, nor will frequent liquid feeding.

If you want some baby aspidistras, the outside leaves can be gently pulled off with a piece of rhizome (creeping stem) and roots attached, and potted in 7.5-cm (3-in) pots in spring.

Brown spots and edges to the leaves usually mean too dry an atmosphere or too much water in the compost, but these conditions have to be really exaggerated before the plant complains.

Peperomias come from tropical areas such as the West Indies and South America, where they grow in the mountains. Most species were introduced in the last century, for greenhouse cultivation. The flowers are unusual and quite different to those of other indoor plants; they are white, narrow, tail-like spikes on pink or red stems, standing straight up above the leaves and sometimes curled over at the tip like an old-fashioned umbrella handle.

Peperomia caperata is the smallest, a bushy little plant about 15 cm (6 in) high, with corrugated leaves. *P. marmorata* (also sold as *P. hederaefolia*) has larger, lighter grey-green leaves, blistered-looking, with dark green veins, and is altogether a larger plant. *P. magnoliaefolia* is much more like a miniature shrub, with a main stem about 30 cm (1 ft) tall, from which the sideshoots and smooth fleshy leaves grow alternately, each up to 15 cm (6 in) long.

A dry atmosphere is death to these plants; they love humidity, and shallow dishes of water, overhead spraying, growing in groups, any or all of these are vital to a peperomia's health. Use John Innes potting compost (see page 8) with half as much peat added, and water only moderately with tepid water, even in summer. Too much water at the root or a dry atmosphere will lead to rotting of the leaf stems at soil level, and the plant gradually and mysteriously diminishes in size until it is not worth growing. The nutrient in the composts should last until the second season when liquid feeding will be necessary.

Keep the temperature not less than 10°C (50°F) in winter and put the plant in a good light at all times. The species *caperata* and *marmorata* grow best in pans, rather than pots.

Leaf cuttings can be used to increase these plants; put the leaf stem in sandy compost up to the base of the leaf, and cover the pot with a plastic bag. Then put the pot in a warm place in the shade. The species *magnoliaefolia* is, however, grown from stem cuttings, removing the shoot tips in the usual way; you must supply warmth for them to root. It is a good idea to use a hormone rooting compound for this one.

The pileas are not difficult to grow. There are two species with plain green leaves and two with variegated, described under 'Variegated Foliage Plants I', but all are quite different. *Pilea involucrata* (syn. *P. pubescens*) is a low compact plant whose corrugated leaves are brownish green and hairy, each pair set crosswise to the pair below it. Slow to grow, it needs plenty of humidity at all times, warmth (at least 7°C (45°F) in winter), a good light and warm water when watering. Use John Innes potting compost (see page 8) with extra sand added, and supply plenty of drainage material. Tip cuttings will root easily in sandy soil. Sometimes the leaves fall late in winter, but if you take cuttings the plant will produce new leafy shoots low down.

Pilea microphylla (syn. *P. muscosa*) is sometimes called the Gunpowder Plant, or Artillery Plant, because its pollen is literally shot out in clouds. The tiny leaves are clustered on the stems so that the plant looks like a dense green bundle of moss. It is easily grown in warmth, with moisture in the air and at the roots.

See also 'Ferns' and 'Palms'.

The tall handsome aspidistra is back in favour again; it contrasts well with Pilea spruceana

Green foliage plants II

Cyperus alternifolius (Umbrella Plant)∗ , *Dizygotheca elegantissima*∗∗ , *Grevillea robusta* (Australian Silk Oak)∗ , *Monstera deliciosa* (Swiss Cheese Plant)∗∗

The attraction of this group of plants lies in the shape of the leaves, rather than in their colouring. All are tall and handsome yet completely different from one another, and you have a choice between perforated, feathery, spidery and umbrella-like leaves. At least one of these should blend with the decoration of a room in your home.

Apart from its name, the Umbrella Plant has another association with water, as it likes to be kept well watered, to the extent of standing in saucers of water during the summer. Actually it is one of the Sedge family, whose long narrow leaves curve over from the top of the stem like the skeleton of an umbrella. It grows to about 60 cm (2 ft) and produces a cluster of stems, so that one plant will have several umbrellas. The feathery flowers, which are typical of the grass family, come from the centre of the umbrellas.

Cool conditions, both summer and winter, suit it, with a little shade and some humidity. Lack of moisture will make the tips of the leaves turn brown, or become infested with red spider mite. Use John Innes potting composts (see page 8), and feed during summer. Increase by dividing the plant in spring.

Dizygotheca elegantissima lives up to its specific name; it is certainly an elegant plant, with toothed narrow leaflets, about seven to a leaf, radiating from a central point. When young, the leaves have a tinge of red, but the adult leaves are very dark green and glossy. It is a native of the New Hebrides near the Fiji Islands and was first introduced as a hothouse plant, but since then has moved into the home.

Dizygotheca is not a beginner's plant; it dislikes draughts, overwatering, great changes in temperature, a dry atmosphere and cold. In other words, it demands a steamy jungle, and you will need to provide conditions as close to this as possible. No less than 10°C (50°F) is needed in winter, and correspondingly high temperatures in summer, but only put the plant in central heating if it can be sprayed regularly every day and given humidity by the shallow dish method (see page 6), otherwise the leaves will drop. They will also fall if the temperature varies, or if the plant becomes badly infested with red spider mite.

Dizygotheca is not so difficult about light, as it will take a little shade or ordinary light, and the usual quantities of water are suitable—a good deal in summer, much less in winter. Liquid feeding once every two weeks during the growing period will be sufficient food, and use the John Innes potting composts (see page 8).

As a house plant it does not often reach more than 60 cm (2 ft)

or so, because by that time it has often lost all its leaves through the wrong care and dies, but it will grow very much taller if treated properly.

Feathery foliage is always charming and, although the Australian Silk Oak is a tree of over 30 m (100 ft) in its native New South Wales, it produces its pinnate, silky green leaves right from the time it is a seedling. Many forest trees grown in pots take too long to leaf to be worth growing, but grevillea, named after C. F. Greville, one of the founders of the Royal Horticultural Society, grows quickly and is evergreen. In Australia the mature tree produces yellow flowers but, sadly, never as a pot plant.

Kept cool in summer (it can go outdoors) and with a temperature of as low as 4°C (40°F) in winter, grevillea is not difficult to grow. It will need John Innes Potting Compost No. 2 or 3 (see page 8), with a little extra sand as it likes good drainage; repot once or twice in a season. Give it a good light at all times and plenty of water in summer, but over- (or under-) watering will make the lower leaves drop. Red spider mite is a common invader and easy to miss, because the leaves already have a tinge of bronze, the sign of red spider feeding, so keep an eye on the underside of the leaves. Overhead spraying will ward off possible attacks.

The Swiss Cheese plant, *Monstera deliciosa*, is actually a climber, but as a pot plant this characteristic is not very noticeable; it tends to grow more as an ordinary tall plant. It has very large leathery leaves, which are deeply incised from the margins; it is said that these indentations, and the holes which later appear, have developed so that the leaves do not subject an unbroken surface to the tremendous gales of its native climate. Whatever the reason, the plant looks most effective with modern furniture and architecture. There is an especially good variety called *M. d.* Variegata, whose leaves are mottled and splashed with cream.

The plant will produce aerial roots from the stems which can be trained on to bark supports, or down into the compost. If the top of the plant is removed to use as a cutting, it will take more quickly if there are aerial roots on it. Cutting off the tip like this also keeps the plant's height under control and will encourage sideshoots to come from lower down.

Monstera is from tropical America, so plenty of warmth, not less than 10°C (50°F) in winter, and humidity at all times are essential; spray the plant every day and keep in a container of water. Regular feeding in summer, and John Innes Potting Compost No. 2 or 3 (see page 8) are also necessary, and you should sponge the leaves to keep them clean and glossy. A well-lit place, but not sunny, and plenty of water in summer will produce good growth.

See also 'Palms' and 'The Fig Family'.

The 'delicious monster', Monstera deliciosa, is an impressive plant needing plenty of space

Variegated foliage plants
I

Aglaonema commutatum (Chinese Evergreen)✹✹ , *Dieffenbachia amoena* (Dumb Cane)✹✹ , *Dracaena godseffiana* Florida Beauty✹✹ , *Peperomia obtusifolia* Variegata✹✹ , *P. glabella* Variegata✹✹ , *Pilea cadierei* (Aluminium Plant)✹ , *P. spruceana* ✹

One of the attractions about growing plants indoors is the variation not only in shape of leaf, but in colour. When house plants first became popular, they were mainly grown for their foliage—flowering plants want a good deal of light, which is difficult to supply in the average home. So the house plant suppliers scoured the world to find as many different kinds of foliage plants for the home as possible. Plain-green-leaved plants certainly have their place in the home where there is already design and colour; patterned leaves will point up a simple setting.

The Chinese Evergreen is not apparently very suitably named as it comes from the Philippines, but at least the leaves are evergreen. They are large, deep green and oval, with a more or less regular pattern of whitish-grey blotches on either side of the veins, making it really rather a handsome plant. During the summer it will be happiest in a slightly shaded place, but in the winter it can be put where the light is good, though not sunny. Constant humidity is essential, especially in winter, if only to keep red spider mite at bay; besides supplying a shallow dish of water, spraying every day is also a good idea. Keep the temperature at the same level during winter, not less than 10°C (50°F), higher if possible, and place the plant away from gas or coal fires, otherwise the leaves brown and drop. Water rather sparingly in winter, and in summer feed every week as well as watering well; John Innes Potting Compost No. 2 or 3 (see page 8) will be needed. If you want to increase it, division in spring is the easiest way. It may flower in July, but the red berries which follow are much more colourful than the flowers.

If you want to stop somebody talking, give them a piece of the leaf of *Dieffenbachia amoena* to chew; the sap is extremely bitter and causes considerable pain—in fact the whole plant is very poisonous, so it is not called the Dumb Cane for nothing. With this warning in mind, it is worth growing for its appearance; its leaves are large, about 23 cm (9 in) long, and much spotted and blotched with white. It was introduced from Brazil in 1820 and named after Herr Dieffenbach, an Austrian gardener at the Imperial Palace in Vienna.

Dieffenbachia will take quite a lot of light, but not summer sun, which burns the leaves. Plenty of humidity is essential, especially in central heating in winter, when the temperature should not drop below 10°C (50°F). It is not a very thirsty plant, but don't let it dry out in winter; you will probably find that it drops one or two leaves, but this is normal, and it will compensate with new growth in spring. It will not tolerate draughts. Compost should be well-drained, as the fleshy roots will rot quickly if they absorb too much water.

There are all sorts of dracaenas, quite different in habit. An exotically named example is *Dracaena draco*, the Dragon Tree from the Canary Islands, said to live for at least 1,000 years; the sticky red liquid produced by the leaves was once believed to be dragon's blood. It can grow to a tree 18 m (60 ft) tall. *D. godseffiana* Florida Beauty is a rather spreading plant, with slender stems and rounded oval leaves, very heavily spotted and blotched with creamy white. It does not grow very quickly. This species comes from the Congo, so warmth and humidity at all times will be needed, plus a good light and fortnightly sponging of the leaves. Watch for greenfly. Keep it in John Innes potting compost (see page 8) and feed it while it is growing. This is one of the plants which can be increased by division in spring; single shoots can be separated off and potted up individually.

Peperomias are discussed under 'Green Foliage Plants I', but there are two other species with yellow- and cream-patterned foliage which are equally ornamental. *Peperomia obtusifolia* Variegata has rounded fleshy leaves, with irregular creamy yellow margins, and thick stems. It grows into a nice bushy plant, and if you take out the tips of the shoots it will be even bushier, and develop at a faster rate. *P. glabella* Variegata naturally grows as a trailing plant, but you can make it bushy by pinching out the tips two or three times while it is growing, as it is a fast worker, and sends out its reddish-stemmed sideshoots very quickly. Some of the slightly pointed leaves will be completely creamy-white; remember that a plant with many of these will not grow so quickly, because of the lack of chlorophyll (green colouring matter) through which the plant makes some of the elements it needs to maintain life.

Both these peperomias will need more light than the plain kind, and be sparing with water, especially in winter. Otherwise they have the same needs as the plain varieties described earlier.

The Aluminium Plant, *Pilea cadierei*, has a distinctly shiny and metallic appearance, with silvery white patches in a herringbone formation on the leaves. These markings are in fact formed by blisters of air between the cells of the plant. It comes from Indo-China and was introduced to France in 1938; all the many thousands of individual plants now grown have come from this single plant, for example, *P. spruceana*, shown opposite.

It is easily grown from 6–7.5-cm (2½–3-in) tip cuttings, kept warm and shaded in a plastic bag. You can use the tips taken off the stems when you pinch it back to make it branch out, which it does very willingly. In fact, it is an easy plant to grow altogether, and, provided it is fed weekly in summer, watered well, and sprayed every day, it will rapidly grow to about 30 cm (12 in) and at least 23 cm (9 in) wide. A dry atmosphere and too much heat will produce leaf drop, also red spider mite. In winter keep the temperature above 7°C (45°F), and water less.

Dieffenbachia amoena, and D. Tropic Snow (centre), Pilea cadierei (on the stove), P. spruceana below it, and Fittonia verschaffeltii argyroneura on the floor

Variegated foliage plants II

Cordyline indivisa∗, C. terminalis∗∗,
Codiaeum variegatum pictum (Croton)∗∗∗

These two plants seem to get rather muddled up in people's minds, mainly because they both have brilliantly coloured leaves on rather upright plants. In fact they belong to quite different plant families, the codiaeums to the euphorbias and the cordylines to the *Agave* family. They do come from the same parts of the world, however, the crotons (codiaeum) from Malaya and the Pacific Islands, and the cordylines from Australasia and Polynesia. It is essential that the codiaeums and *Cordyline terminalis* have constant warmth and humidity, but *C. indivisa* is much less demanding and will even grow out of doors in mild gardens.

The word 'codiaeum' comes from the native name for the plant, *kodiho*, and in tropical countries they are good plants for hedges and borders. They reach a height of about 1.2 m (4 ft) but grow rather slowly. As with any member of the euphorbia family, they exude a white sticky sap and if you are taking cuttings this should be stopped with powdered charcoal or cigarette ash, otherwise the prolonged 'bleeding' weakens them.

Their leaves are fantastically brilliant in colour, and they catch the eye in a florist's window before any of the other plants. Some varieties have long oval-shaped leathery leaves, others are long and narrow and yet others are lobed. Although some green, usually a bright emerald, is often present on the leaves, other colours include orange, yellow, pink, red, dark green and dark (almost black) red, either outlining the veins or as spots and blotches. Some of the more commonly seen colourings are combinations of green and yellow, yellow-spotted on green with red veins, orange with pink blotches and so on, but there is tremendous variation and no two plants are alike. All this showiness needs very careful handling, however.

One of the most important points is to keep the temperature up and at the same level. As soon as the temperature changes, even if it goes back to the original level fairly quickly, or if it drops permanently, the leaves will fall, starting at the bottom, and you will very quickly be left with nothing but a bare stem. So it is worth taking some extra care to prevent this happening, especially as these plants are not cheap.

The winter temperature therefore should not fall below 13°C (55°F), and, whatever degree of warmth is given, it is important to keep it constant and to prevent draughts. At the same time humidity must be provided, both by permanently evaporating water and by misting the leaves daily. Give the plant as much light as possible, including sunlight unless very intense, as this ensures that the leaves keep their colour. If your plant tries to flower, remove the buds before they open so that all the plant's energies are directed into the leaf growth.

If by any sad chance the leaves do fall, cut the main stem back to about 15 cm (6 in); with the help of a little extra heat new growth should come from the base. You can use the top of the part cut off as a cutting about 10 cm (4 in) long, rooting it in a temperature of about 21°C (70°F). A weak liquid feed every seven days while growing, and John Innes potting composts (see page 8) are suitable. Remember that the end of the cutting and the top of the main stem will need to be treated to stop bleeding. Watch out for red spider mite.

The cordylines, being members of the *Agave* family, can be distinguished from the codiaeums by the arrangement of the veins in the leaves. Flowering plants are divided into two main groups, botanically speaking; in the first group, one characteristic is that the leaf veins branch out to form a network from a central main vein which extends the length of the leaf. In the second group, which includes the grasses and the orchids as well as lilies, iris and so on, the veins are usually parallel, mostly from the base of the leaf at the point where the stem is attached; in only a few genera are they net-like. If you look at a cordyline leaf, you will see this parallel veining quite clearly.

One sometimes feels that the plant collectors were rather at a loss to name their new plants; cordyline was so called from the Greek *kordyle*, meaning a club, in reference to the shape of the roots of some species (the root of *C. terminalis* is edible and used to be eaten by the Maoris). There must, however, be many plants with similarly shaped roots.

Cordyline indivisa has long narrow dark green leaves with a red midrib, which spray out and downwards from a central stem. Outdoors it can grow into a tree of 7.5 m (25 ft), but in a pot it probably will not be more than 60 or 90 cm (2 or 3 ft). In the mildest gardens it will grow outdoors.

Cordyline likes a winter temperature of 7°C (45°F) and a normal summer temperature. Keep it in a humid atmosphere, give it a good light, water normally and feed occasionally. A very humus-rich compost is best.

Cordyline terminalis is much more brightly coloured and correspondingly less easy to care for; to look at it is rather like a brightly coloured aspidistra. The large 30-cm-(1-ft)-long leaves are blotched and splashed with various shades of pink, rose pink, purple, cerise, wine red and so on, with cream and white mixed in on a background of medium to dark green. It is an extremely handsome plant and there are many different named varieties. Some plants have leaves completely covered in colour without any of the normal green present at all; they really are exotic, and are a delight to have in a plant display.

In its native tropical Asia, this cordyline is a shrub up to 4 m (12 ft) tall, but pot plants will probably only grow to 60 or 90 cm (2 or 3 ft), unless they are being grown in a large display.

Temperatures of 10°C (50°F) in winter are needed, and humidity, plus regular misting and once weekly sponging of the leaves, is advisable. Put the plant in a good light, but with shade from summer sun. Water well in summer, feed regularly and repot in John Innes potting composts with extra peat mixed in. Watch for red spider mite and greenfly. Increase by tip cuttings or try root cuttings, using pieces of fleshy roots buried in a mixture of sand and peat and kept at 24°C (75°F).

See also Coleus under 'Throwaway Plants'.

Varieties of the croton, Codiaeum variegatum pictum, whose leaves are brighter than many flowers

Variegated foliage plants III

Dracaena deremensis ✳✳ , *D. sanderiana* ✳✳ , *D. fragrans* ✳✳ ,
Sansevieria trifasciata (Mother-in-law's Tongue, Snake Plant) ✳ ,
Scindapsus aureus (Devil's Ivy) ✳✳ , *Syngonium* (*Nephthytis*)
podophyllum (Goosefoot Plant) ✳✳

Common names of house plants are nothing if not varied; only one of this group, the dracaena, has no specific common name, although the umbrella name for its genus is the Dragon Plant. The common names of the others are certainly picturesque and descriptive! These are all tall plants whose green leaves are lightened by shades of yellow; they are good for growing in plant arrangements to break up an otherwise rather flat grouping, whether in troughs or circular containers. A corner by a window is often a good place, whereas a bushy plant like an aspidistra might take up too much room.

The handsome *Draceana sanderiana* has slender stems and rather narrow leaves with creamy-white edges and greyish green centres. It can become rather lanky and even lose some leaves at the bottom, but by the time it reaches this stage it will have produced sideshoots low down so that the bare stems will not be obvious. Hailing from the Congo, it is less tender than one might expect, but it does like humidity, and a winter temperature of not less than 10°C (50°F). Plenty of light all year will prevent the variegation from fading; don't overwater in summer, and use the John Innes potting composts (see page 8) for repotting. *D. deremensis* has a similar habit of growth; its narrow dark green leaves are longitudinally striped with white. Bausei is an attractive variety of it.

Dracaena fragrans lindenii is quite different in appearance; while young it gives the impression of being rather bushy, but it gradually elongates as it grows older—in the wild it is a 4.5–6-m (15–20-ft) tree. The leaves can be as much as 10 cm (4 in) wide, with a broad yellow edge and narrow green and yellow longitudinal stripes in the centre. Give it the same treatment as *D. sanderiana*, but in addition sponge the leaves weekly.

Sansevieria trifasciata has the common names of Snake Plant and Mother-in-law's Tongue; neither seems to be very appropriate, and it might be better called the Hemp Plant. Many species are grown as a commercial crop in India and other hot countries for their fine but strong white fibres, which are woven into mats, twine, rope and hats.

It is a native of West Tropical Africa and belongs to the Lily family, but don't expect conventional lily-like flowers if your plant ever reaches the flowering stage. Warmth, humidity, good light and feeding will encourage a few flowering spikes in summer, on stems 60 cm (2 ft) or so tall. The flowers will be green or greenish-white, but they are rare in cultivation.

Sansevieria t. Laurentii has yellow edges to its stiff fleshy leaves, which can grow in a clump up to 1.2 m (4 ft) tall. If you want to increase it, pot one of the baby plants which will be produced by its thick creeping roots; spring is a good time to do this. It will root from leaf cuttings taken in summer by simply chopping a leaf crosswise into sections and rooting them in warm sandy compost, but the new plants will have green leaves without the yellow edges.

Sansevierias will put up with nearly as much neglect as aspidistras; central heating and dry air, drought, sun or shade are all one to them, but too much watering in winter, particularly if the temperature is low, will very quickly rot the leaves at soil level. Water very sparingly then, as little as once a month; even in summer only moderate watering is needed. Temperatures in winter can be 10°C (50°F), or even 7°C (45°F), with very little watering, but a temperature as low as this is not really advisable.

Strictly speaking, *Scindapsus aureus*, the Devil's Ivy, should not be amongst this group as it is a climbing plant, but pinching out the tips will control its growth so that it is merely tall, and somewhat branching, rather than climbing. It is from the Solomon Islands but in spite of this will take a winter temperature as low as 10°C (50°F).

The stems are fleshy and the leaves light green, spotted and streaked yellow. The variety Marble Queen is quite outstanding, with leaves very heavily marked in white—some are completely white—and others barely flecked with green. If you grow this plant trained against bark or a sphagnum moss pad, it will attach itself by aerial roots and the leaves will be very much larger.

Light is essential if the variegations are to be retained; humidity is also vital, including spraying overhead daily in summer. Plenty of water is needed in summer, but not in winter; too much at this time will brown the leaves and rotting will set in. Liquid feed while growing and use the standard composts for repotting. Draughts and gas in the atmosphere will discolour the leaves and check the plant's growth. Tip cuttings root easily in water or potting compost, given warmth, but choose shoots which are well-variegated for the most ornamental plants.

The Goosefoot Plant is so-named because it has leaves shaped rather like a goose's foot, with three lobes—one long central one, and smaller ones at each side. The veins are outlined in white in the variety *albolineatum*, emphasizing the attractive shape of the leaves, and as several stems are produced from the crown, it tends to form a tall bushy plant, especially if the tips are pinched out in the same way as scindapsus (above). Like that plant, it is also a climber, but it is generally grown as a tall plant rather than for its twining ability.

Syngonium comes from Central America and is one of the aroids, a group of plants which produce trailing aerial roots in suitably humid conditions, and it will therefore take kindly to a bark or sphagnum moss support. Keep it watered, but not too much, otherwise the leaves turn yellow and fall. Draughts and sudden changes of temperature are also unpopular, and while it is resting the temperature should not drop below 10°C (50°F). A John Innes potting compost (see page 8) with extra peat will give its roots the additional air they need, and feeding every ten days or so will keep up the nourishment. A slightly shaded position is best, but it will grow in most degrees of light except direct shade or hot sun.

See also Abutilon, Aphelandra and 'The Fig Family'.

Sansevieria trifasciata Laurentii (back), Dracaena Souvenir de Schriever (centre), D. deremensis Bausei (front) and D. Tricolor (right)

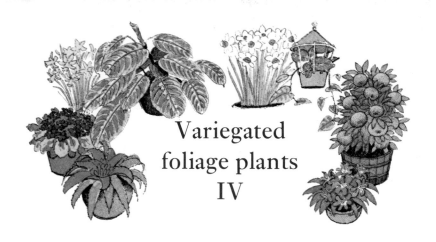

Variegated foliage plants IV

Calathea makoyana (Peacock Plant)∗∗∗ , *Hypoestes sanguinolenta* (Spotted Dog, Polka Dot Plant, Freckle Face)∗ , *Iresine herbstii*∗ , *Maranta leuconeura* (Prayer Plant, Ten Commandment Plant)∗∗∗

To provide colour in the home, plants are usually grown for their flowers, but there are also many plants which have strikingly coloured leaves. As well as those plants with yellow and white variegations mentioned above, there are plants with red, orange, magenta, pink, brown and purple markings.

One of the most richly coloured is the Peacock Plant, *Calathea makoyana*. The leaves are a delightful mixture of pale and dark green, silvery white and wine red. They are large and egg-shaped, with markings on the upper side which are a cross between herring-bone and feathery. The reddish colouring is on the undersurface but it does show through, and the stems are also red-coloured. The whole plant can grow to about 1.2 m (4 ft) tall, but unfortunately most pot specimens only grow to a maximum height of 30 cm (12 in), after which they die as a result of being wrongly looked after.

This species of calathea is a native of Brazil, where it grows in very warm and very humid conditions. In winter the temperature should not drop below 30°C (55°F), preferably higher, but at the same time it is essential to keep the air round the leaves really moist, especially in central heating. If the plant is allowed to become dry, the leaves will curl up and brown and wither, and this happens quite quickly. So misting every day should be automatic, and if you can supply humidifiers as well, so much the better. Otherwise use the shallow dish method (see page 6).

Being a forest plant, calathea needs some shade; sun will bleach the intensity of the colours. Watering should be reasonably plentiful in summer, but be careful, because it is slow to grow; much less water is needed in winter. Feed regularly while the plant is growing, and use a compost with plenty of peat or leaf-mould in it and coarse sand for drainage, so that it is moist but not waterlogged, otherwise the roots will rot. One of the best ways of growing this plant is in a bottle garden (see under 'Terrariums and Bottle Gardens').

Hypoestes sanguinolenta, the Spotted Dog Plant, is a fairly recent addition to the selection of plants for the home, and is turning out to be very successful. It is not difficult to grow, and the pink to white spots on the leaves are unique. The plant originally comes from Madagascar and can grow to about 45 cm (18 in) tall, with leaves up to 7.5 cm (3 in) long on slender stems. In the wild it has pale purple flowers, but they are not conspicuous and are only seen in the home when the plant has been allowed to become straggly.

A good light will preserve the pinkness of the spots, but too much light or sunlight will bleach them white. Water the plant well while it is growing, but very much less while it is just 'ticking over' during its resting period. Taking out the tips of the shoots in spring and summer will keep it nicely compact and more leafy; some humidity is necessary, and the temperature in winter should not be lower than 10°C (50°F). Feed with a nitrogen-high fertilizer once a fortnight and use the John Innes potting composts (see page 8) for spring repotting, if necessary. Increase by means of the tip cuttings put into sandy compost and keep warm and humid; they root quickly and easily. Watch out for scale insects, which can be a nuisance with this plant.

Iresine herbstii used to be much grown as an outdoor bedding plant, for summer planting only as it is not hardy, but it also makes a good pot plant. The wine-purple, rounded leaves and stems have contrasting lighter red veins. It arrived from South America in 1864 and was promptly snapped up by the Victorians for their highly geometric and formal plantings; it is still much grown in the Canary Islands in this way.

Iresine makes a good foil for plain green-leaved plants or it can be mixed with red- and flame-coloured foliage plants for a really dazzling display. As a centrepiece for a plant group, it can hold its own with any flowering plant.

Not difficult to grow, its main requirement is warmth in winter and plenty of water in summer, provided the compost is well drained, with extra coarse sand in it and broken pottery at the bottom of the pot. In winter give much less water, just enough to keep the soil moist. Repot in early spring, and at the same time pinch out the tips if the plant is getting straggly. It will take any amount of light, even sunlight, but keep the atmosphere moist. Cuttings 7.5 cm (3 in) long will root quickly in compost or water.

The marantas are closely related to the calatheas, but on the whole are rather smaller plants. *Maranta leuconeura* is called the Prayer Plant because the leaves have a peculiar habit: in the daytime they lie flat, but as evening comes they gradually lift up until they are erect and closed, like hands folded in prayer. In the wild this is done to retain water during the night.

From this behaviour it is easy to see that marantas have a great need for humidity, and they should be misted at least daily. Without humidity the leaves very quickly turn brown at the tips, eventually drying up completely so that the whole plant is spoilt.

The variety of *Maranta leuconeura* called *kerchoveana* has emerald green leaves with purple blotches between the side veins symmetrically placed in herring-bone formation, usually five to a side. The average height is about 30 cm (1 ft), but the leaves are surprisingly large for such a comparatively small plant, up to 15 cm (6 in) in length. The genus is named after S. Maranti, a Venetian botanist of the mid-sixteenth century, and the species was introduced from Brazil in 1875.

The other variety often sold is *massangeana*, with rather technicoloured leaves. The herring-bone veins are white, coming from the central midrib, which is itself outlined in light green; the rest of the leaf is dark green on top except for magenta blotches which are not, however, so obvious as in *kerchoveana*, and the underneath is wine red.

Besides humidity, marantas love warmth (like many humans) and in winter the temperature should ideally not be lower than 13°C (55°F). Place the plant out of draughts, and in the shade. Give it very little water in winter, and only water moderately in summer; it needs a weak feed once every seven days while it is growing and, if you can, grow it in pans. The plants may flower in summer but the small white blossoms are not particularly attractive. Marantas can be increased by dividing in spring, removing any dead or damaged leaves at the same time.

See also 'Foliage Begonias', Impatiens, 'Throwaway Plants' and 'Pelargoniums'.

Calathea makoyana, Maranta leuconeura kerchoveana (centre), and M. l. Tricolor (with red veins)

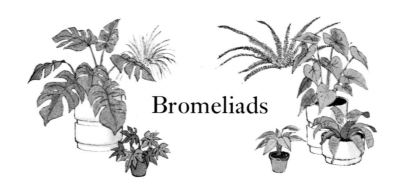

Bromeliads

Aechmea fasciata (Urn Plant)* , *Billbergia nutans** , *Cryptanthus* spp. (Earth Star)* , *Tillandsia* spp. (Blue Bromeliad and Spanish Moss)** , *Vriesea splendens***

Though you have probably not realized it, you have doubtless eaten a bromeliad. One of our most delicious fruits belongs to this family—that large dull orange object with a tuft of stiff green leaves on top, the pineapple. Several members of this plant family have the same type of fruit, but they are not often produced in cultivation.

The bromeliads are exotic plants, natives of both Central and South America, particularly the tropical areas, but in spite of this they do not necessarily insist on very high temperatures. Some will accept a temperature of as low as 7°C (45°F) during their resting period, but what they seem to want is warmth in their growing season, while they are still offsets, if they are to flower the following year.

They are quite different in appearance to most other plants, as they consist of an elongated rosette of stiff, strap-shaped leaves, which forms a kind of funnel or 'vase' out of the centre of which comes the flower stem and a very curious flowerhead. The main attraction of this is usually the coloured bracts, which form a cone, a sheath or a gracefully hanging cluster, from which emerge the smallish flowers, often in a brilliant and contrasting colour to the bracts. The flowerheads can last for months, though the flowers will die after a few weeks. The leaves are plain green, striped horizontally with dark brown or red, and longitudinally with cream and/or pink; in one species, *Aechmea fasciata*, they are grey-green with silvery bands.

Bromeliads are mostly epiphytes, in other words they perch on objects above the ground, usually trees. Instead of growing them in the conventional pots, you could try attaching them to dead branches, lengths of bark bound with sphagnum moss, or rocks and stones. Their root system is small, and mainly for anchoring the plant. Water and some nutrient is absorbed through the roots, but water is also taken in through the 'vase' which should be kept topped up with tepid water (preferably rainwater), even though the flower stem comes straight up through it. You can occasionally give a little weak liquid fertilizer via the vase as well, but be careful not to overdo it.

The general care of bromeliads is as follows; for different requirements for individual plants see below. The compost should be very rich in humus without any soil in it, for instance equal parts of peat and leaf-mould with half a part of coarse sand. Keep this moist but by no means saturated during the growing season, and just damp when the plant is resting in winter. The water in the 'vase' should be kept as full as possible without overflowing; even while the plant is resting, it should still contain some water. Give the plants as much light as possible, with the exception of direct hot sunlight; some humidity is also appreciated. Bromeliads like normal temperatures in spring and summer, but not lower than 7°C (45°F) in dormancy, 10°C (50°F) for some kinds, as mentioned below.

Aechmea fasciata, the Urn Plant, is one of the most well-known bromeliads. It is one of the most charming in its colouring, with silver-white-striped, grey-green leaves, a bright pink cone-shaped flowerhead, and blue flowers. The flowerhead will last up to six months, appearing first in late May. Aechmea will stand the dry atmosphere of central heating (although it will be better for some humidity), and quite low temperatures in winter down to 7°C (45°F). It will grow as large as 45 cm (18 in) wide and 30 cm (12 in) high.

Billbergia nutans has dangling flowers which push out from bright pink bracts; the flowers are navy blue, yellow and green, appearing in late spring and early summer and lasting for several weeks. The leaves are narrow, slightly spiny at the edges and end in a point. This bromeliad is one of the terrestrial kind, and will therefore take a little soil in the compost; it particularly likes good drainage, so plenty of broken pottery at the bottom of the container will be needed. Too much light will turn the leaves yellow-green, but otherwise it is very hardy.

The *Cryptanthus* species, the Earth Stars, are rather like starfish to look at; the leaves fan out flat and close to the ground from the central 'vase'. The plants vary in size from a few centimetres wide to almost 30 cm (12 in). Horizontal stripes of whitish grey and dark red-green colour the wavy leaves of *C. fosterianus* if it is put in a good light, but in shade it tends to lose the distinctive striping and becomes dark and light green. *C. bivittatus* is smaller and flatter; its dark green leaves have a broad creamy stripe lengthways down the edges, flushed rose-pink in bright light.

The plant sometimes known as the Blue Bromeliad is *Tillandsia cyanea*, most exotically coloured. The leaves are long and narrow, produced in rather grass-like profusion, but it is for the flowerhead that the plant is grown. The bracts are bright pink, forming a flattened cone, and brilliant blue, comparatively large flowers come out from between the bracts; each flower lasts a few days and the whole spike is in flower for about two months from early June. The size of the plant is about 30 cm (12 in) tall and 45 cm (18 in) wide. Without a good light, it may not flower at all and it does like humidity, but it will survive fairly low temperatures.

The Blue Bromeliad's relative *T. usneoides* is totally unlike it; its common name is Spanish Moss or Old Man's Beard. It hangs down in long, grey hair-like clusters, up to 6 m (20 ft) long, and needs no soil, simply rooting on bare branches; humidity is very important.

Vriesea splendens has a brilliant scarlet sword-like flowerhead about 60 cm (24 in) tall, carrying bright yellow, short-lived flowers. The leaves form the usual 'vase' and are horizontally banded in dark brown, though this colouring fades a little when the flowers appear. Keep the temperature up in winter, 10°C (50°F), and give this bromeliad humidity—it can't do without it. Sponging the leaves occasionally will be appreciated.

All these bromeliads can be increased very simply and easily by using the offsets produced at the base of the plant. These, together with their roots, can be detached when they are about 15 cm (6 in) tall and potted up in late spring in 7.5-cm (3-in) pots, using the usual humus-rich mixture of peat, sphagnum moss and leafmould. They will need to be kept in quite a high temperature, between 21° and 27°C (70° and 80°F), until they are established.

Cryptanthus Tricolor and C. fosterianus (in front) are different kinds of Earth Stars

Fragrant plants

Exacum affine*, Gardenia***, *Iris reticulata**,
Jasminum polyanthum (Jasmine)*

Fragrant plants have an indefinable magic about them, which is always welcome indoors.

Exacum affine has no common name, although it is very easy to care for. From Socotra, an island in the Gulf of Aden, it is a small bushy plant, which can be had in flower from June until the end of October. Exacum is a biennial, but it can also be grown as a half-hardy annual; it is a 'throwaway' plant, but it flowers so profusely and for so long, as well as being fragrant, that it is very much worth growing.

The flowers are purple with yellow centres, and new buds are constantly produced to take the place of the dying blooms. The whole plant is about 23 cm (9 in) tall, compact and well-leafed. Flowering plants are available from florists in the summer but if you want to grow your own you should sow the seed in early September in a temperature of 16°C (60°F). Growing the plants on is rather a fiddly business without a greenhouse, but it can be done. The seedlings should be pricked out and, when large enough, put into 7.5-cm (3-in) pots, where they remain for the winter. This is when care becomes a little difficult, as they need to be kept at about 13°C (55°F), more if possible. It is important that this temperature is kept constant. In spring put the plants into 12-cm (5-in) pots to flower. An easier method of producing flowering plants is to use exactly the same process but starting much later, in March; flowering will then start in August and continue until late October.

While the plants are growing, they like warmth, some humidity, and shade from very hot sun. If the leaves begin to turn brown at the tips and the flowers die quickly, this is a sign that they are getting too much sun. Only moderate watering is required, but liquid feeding every week is necessary, using a feed with a high potash content because of the flowers. (See also 'Throwaway Plants'.)

Jasmine is heavily fragrant and flowers continuously for most of the summer. The white, pink-flushed flowers are about 2 cm (¾ in) long and grow in clusters. *Jasminum polyanthum* was introduced from China in 1891. It is a climbing shrub with attractively pinnate leaves, and will be evergreen in the house.

Jasmine should have as much light as possible if it is to flower indoors; it gets very straggly without enough light, and will not produce flowers. But if the sun gets very hot, move it temporarily. The plant grows fast in spring and summer, and will need strong supports; to reduce the height, you can train it round circles of cane or wire. Any pruning, to shape or to reduce the size, should be done in late February.

Water the plant moderately during growing and flowering, much less in winter. Keep it on the cool side in winter, though free from frost; it may drop some leaves, but this is natural. Moderate humidity is required, and feeding about once every two weeks from mid-July onwards. This is one of the plants that flowers better if potbound; too much space and too rich feeding will produce leafy rather than flowery growth. If it sheds its buds, suspect your watering, draughts or red spider mite.

Jasmine is easily increased from stem cuttings, using the new shoots. The cuttings should be about 15 cm (6 in) long, still soft at the tip but tougher at the other end; take them in July or August. Put them singly into 7.5-cm (3-in) pots for the winter, and then as they grow pot them on into larger ones, up to about 17 cm (7 in), using the John Innes potting composts (see page 8). (See also 'Flowering Climbing Plants'.)

Iris reticulata is a miniature bulb which flowers during winter. It only grows to a height of about 15 cm (6 in) so several plants can be grown in quite a small space. The flowers are deep purple with orange tongues, and are unexpectedly fragrant; they last for several weeks. Plant the bulbs in late August, using John Innes potting compost (see page 8) with extra sand added; they should be about 3.5 cm (1½ in) deep. You can use pans, or small troughs about 11 cm (4½ in) deep—anything larger will overwhelm them. Leave them outdoors in a cool shady place until early October, making sure they do not dry out. When you bring them in, keep them cool, as too much warmth too soon can result in no flowers. As the leaves start to show through, give them as much light as possible, otherwise the plants will be all leaf with very short-stemmed flowers.

After flowering, continue watering and feed regularly until the leaves yellow at the tips, then gradually dry the plants off and put them in a warm place to ripen. You should have new bulbs for the following year, if you have fed and ripened the plants properly. (See also 'Miniature Indoor Bulbs'.)

The gardenia is more often thought of as a greenhouse, even a hothouse, plant, but it is no more demanding than, for example, the codiaeum or maranta, in fact probably easier to grow than the latter. Its white flowers, like a camellia in shape, are strongly fragrant—their perfume will fill a room. They are not produced all at once, but singly one after the other. The gardenia is a shrub, with glossy evergreen leaves, and is named after a Dr Garden, who lived in Carolina during the eighteenth century. He was a friend of the Swedish botanist Linnaeus, who invented the system of naming plants that we now use.

The main difficulty with a house-grown gardenia is its inclination to drop its flower buds; 'beautiful but temperamental' sums up this plant. Too much or too little water, changes of temperature, too much feeding, sudden drying of the compost will all affect it, and the right care can only be learnt from experience. Watering in particular is very much poised on a knife edge. One can only recommend watering reasonably freely when the plant is growing and flowering, and then giving very little water during the dormant season, just enough to keep the soil barely moist. If the leaves begin to yellow and the compost is very moist, stop watering until the plant is nearly completely dry, and be very careful with the quantity in future. Yellowing may also be due to iron deficiency, first noticeable on the top leaves; if so, water with an iron chelate (sequestered iron) solution.

Supply a humid atmosphere, especially in central heating, and mist the plant every day; give a good light, and a temperature of no lower than 13°C (55°F) in winter, preferably 16°C (60°F). An all-year temperature of 18–21°C (65–70°F) is good. Feed regularly when the rounded flower buds start to appear, which will be between June and September, though ideal care will have it flowering most of the year. John Innes potting composts (see page 8) with extra peat are suitable. Watch for red spider mite and scale insects.

The gardenia will perfume an entire room with its hothouse-like fragrance

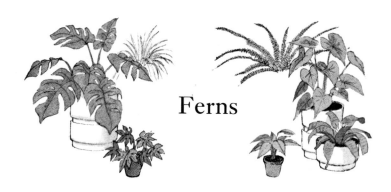

Ferns

Adiantum capillus-veneris (Maidenhair Fern)∗∗ ,
Asparagus setaceus nanus∗ , *A. densiflorus* Sprengeri∗ ,
Asplenium nidus (Bird's Nest Fern)∗∗ , *Cyrtomium falcatum* Holly
Fern∗ , *Platycerium alcicorne* (Stag's Horn Fern)∗∗ ,
Pteris cretica Albo-lineata∗

Ferns are plants which seem to go naturally with mountain streams, rocks, moss and cool shady places, but there are a good many which are in fact used to tropical climates. Though conditions may still be shady, they are far from cool—more like a Turkish bath, in fact.

The Maidenhair Fern, *Adiantum capillus veneris*, is a cosmopolitan and requires a little warmth in winter, humidity all the year round and a copious supply of water, particularly when the temperature rises in summer. It can dry out very quickly and unexpectedly then, so have a look at it every day. Sun will make the leaves shrivel and wither from the edges—they are very delicate and fragile, though the stems are quite wiry. On the whole, the plant is best out of the sun and on the cool side.

Adiantum is a pretty and graceful fern with light green leaves; there are a variety of forms, for instance with crested fronds, more deeply cut leaves, drooping kinds, one which is dwarf, another with curled leaflets, and so on.

Use a John Innes potting compost (see page 8) with extra peat mixed in and rainwater for watering and overhead spraying, as a neutral to acid compost is preferred. Small plants are least able to resist leaf withering, so it pays to obtain one of the larger plants. A little dilute fertilizer once a week in summer is advisable. Draughts and fumes, whether smoke or gas, will damage it.

When you have got the knack of looking after the plant, it can be divided in early spring to produce several smaller plants. You will probably also find, if you have got the growing conditions right, that the spores will germinate on the surface of the compost, and you will have lots of tiny plants which can be grown on.

The ordinary edible asparagus of gardens, derived from *A. officinalis*, if left to grow to its full height will produce the feathery fern so much used by florists for buttonholes, wedding bouquets and other festive floral arrangements. The plant specially grown for this use is a dwarf form, however, called *A. setaceus nanus*, which is more suited to house conditions.

The asparagus fern should not be mollycoddled, but will do best in cool conditions, with a good light. The John Innes potting composts (see page 8) can be used, and an occasional feed while the plant is growing will do no harm. If it is grown in central heating, overhead spraying in winter will be necessary, with some humidity at all times. Water the roots sparingly in winter.

The name in the trade for asparagus fern is sparrow-grass (or even just 'grass'). It used to grow wild on the steppes of Siberia and Eastern Europe.

Asparagus densiflorus Sprengeri produces slender climbing stems up to 1.8 m (6 ft) long. The leaves consist of needle-like leaflets, almost giving the impression of grass growing along the stems. The sprays are very decorative as table decorations.

Like the asparagus fern, it is evergreen, but needs a lower temperature; it likes cool conditions, away from central heating, and some humidity is advisable all year. Water and feed while the plant is growing but stop feeding it in the rest period and water

sparingly. The compost should be well supplied with food. Either shade or a good light are suitable, and you can increase by dividing the plant in spring, when repotting.

The Bird's Nest Fern, *Asplenium nidus*, has undivided, glossy fronds more like ordinary leaves, which can grow to 120 cm (4 ft) long. It is an epiphytic fern which comes from the tropical forests of the Old World. One species of this genus was once considered useful in curing diseases of the spleen, and the common name for the genus is Spleenwort. Give it warmth, humidity, shade and a peaty compost, water freely in summer, and feed all year, though less in winter. Sponge or spray the leaves frequently.

The Holly Fern, *Cyrtomium falcatum*, comes from Japan and the Far East. It is almost hardy, and has glossy leathery fronds, sharply toothed. It is a good fern for indoor use, as it will stand smoke and draughts, and the temperature can drop to 4°C (40°F) in winter. Plenty of water in summer, much less in winter, some humidity and shade all year, and feeding in summer will keep it in good health. Increase by division in early spring.

One of the ferns which requires a good deal of warmth and humidity is the Stag's Horn, *Platycerium alcicorne*. It is a native of Australia, and the name is derived from the Greek *platys*, broad, and *keros*, horn. Its appearance is spectacular; the large, thick, light green leaves grow more or less vertically and are divided at the ends. The young leaves have a grey, cobweb-like coating, which disappears gradually with age. These extraordinary leaves come straight out of a light brown papery 'ball', which is in fact a collection of more leaves, green when young, overlapping at the base of the plant. The plants anchor themselves with these to perch on the trunks of trees and in the forks of branches high above ground.

Being an epiphyte, the Stag's Horn Fern does not need the conventional composts, and is happier in a mixture of moist peat and sphagnum moss, with some rotted manure added, or a little fertilizer powder. It can be grown in a shallow pot or attached to a length of cork bark or dead branch.

The plant likes a light position, but not sunlight, and plenty of humidity is essential. Misting is a good idea, but do not use sprays, which would damage the mealy coating on the young leaves. Summer temperatures in the 70's F will suit it and in winter a temperature of at least 7°C (45°F) should be maintained, 10°C (50°F) if possible. Platycerium needs plenty of water in the higher summer temperatures, and if you are growing it on bark or hanging wood, it is best to take it down and soak it in a container of water, then leave it until it finishes dripping; even with this method there is the problem of the brown leaves at the base which tend to extend all over the top of the pot, so that it is difficult to get the water in.

Increase is by splitting if you have a large plant, but commercially plants are grown from the spores produced on the large, divided fronds.

Pteris cretica Albo-lineata is a pretty feathery fern, with narrow fronds centred with white. The name comes from the Greek *pteron*, a wing, and it will do well in a compost of equal parts loam, leafmould, peat and sand, in shade and humidity, with plenty of water and feeding in summer. The temperature should not fall lower than 7–10°C (45–50°F) in winter, moderately warm in summer.

The Maidenhair Fern, Adiantum capillus-veneris, is an elegant plant for hall or landing

Palms

Chamaedorea elegans Bella✻ , *Chamaerops humilis*✻ ,
Chrysalidocarpus lutescens (Butterfly Palm)✻ , *Cycas revoluta*✻
Howeia forsteriana (Kentia Palm)✻ , *Livistona australis*✻✻ ,
Phoenix canariensis✻

The family of palms is one of the most important to man; various parts of various species can be used for supplying fibres for ropes, for oil and wax, material for baskets, roof thatching and building, betel-nuts, alcoholic liquids and so on. The palms are a tropical family and, because they grow in areas where the sunlight is very intense, they tend to have a thick waxy covering on the leaves which prevents them from giving off moisture quickly.

Although many palms grow to 30 m (100 ft) and more in their home countries, there are some kinds which remain small or grow sufficiently slowly to be worth treating as pot plants. Some produce enormous leaves, up to 12 m (40 ft) in length, others less than 30 cm (1 ft). The leaves can be one of two different shapes, feathery or fan-like, but whatever the shape, they are recognizably palm leaves.

As well as being decorative, palms provide a slightly exotic look, in a way that few of the other indoor plants do. Combine them in a group with hibiscus, passionflowers and a monstera or two, and you have your own South Sea island in the living room (with a little extra heat, and a sunray lamp discreetly hidden).

There is one palm which is a native of Europe: *Chamaerops humilis*, which you will see all round the shores of the Mediterranean, from Spain to Sicily and across to North Africa. It can be grown out of doors in mild sheltered places, and requires less warmth in winter than most of the other species.

Palms are not difficult to grow in the house, provided you cater for their special requirements, slightly different to those of other indoor plants. They tend to grow rather long roots, and if these are damaged, or cut when repotting, the plants take a long time to re-establish and may even die. Because of this arose the tradition of using 'palm pots', which are much deeper in proportion to their width than normal pots. When the plant is young, it grows better if it is slightly crowded in the pot; the new pot should be only just larger than the root ball, and the plant can be left in it until the soil ball is really full of roots. Older plants do not need to be so cramped; they should be repotted into a larger pot which gives a space all round of about 5 cm (2 in).

Several pieces of broken pottery at the bottom of the pot are necessary, even with plastic containers, and you should use a really well-drained compost. The plant will also need to be potted firmly, using a rammer with the larger specimens; be careful not to bury any of the stem, otherwise it will rot.

Plenty of water is essential in the growing season, and quite high temperatures. Although the leaves have their thick waxy covering to retain moisture, humidity is still important, especially in winter central heating, when it is vital. Without it, the leaflets brown at the tips and can wither very quickly, so overhead spraying is advisable. Winter temperatures should not drop below about 10°C (50°F), though chamaerops and howeia will take 7°C (45°F), but remember the rule for winter watering—

the lower the temperature, the less water. Palms should never become completely dry in winter; the compost should be moist enough to keep them ticking over.

Palms will grow in light or shady places, though the best position is probably one which is slightly shaded. Composts can be one of the John Innes potting composts (see page 8), or can consist of equal parts of loam, peat and coarse sand; feeding once a week during the summer growing period is helpful, though there are exceptions to this (see below). The leaves will be all the better for occasional sponging to remove dust and possibly scale insects, which are partial to palms. Increase is usually by seeds but, with the exception of the date palm, this is not usually easy in the home without very high temperatures.

Chamaerops humilis, the European palm, has fan-shaped, pleated leaves, and as it naturally grows to only about 2.4 m (8 ft) it is a good plant for the home. It tends to produce several stems at soil level rather than a single trunk, creating a rather bushy plant with palm-like leaves. Drainage is particularly important. It is possible to increase this palm from suckers, when these are produced.

The Kentia Palm, *Howeia forsteriana*, is probably the most frequently grown palm, with elegant pinnate leaves on slender stems. It is easy to grow and will be satisfied with a winter temperature of 7°C (45°F). Use lime-free water and foliar feed for the best results.

Livistona australis is one of the palms with fan-shaped, rather rounded leaves. It needs a fairly rich compost; if you can add some rotted farm manure this will be ideal. It also likes to be warm at night and the temperature should not fall much below that of the day, and, in any case during winter, not below 10°C (50°F). Scale insect can be even more of a bother than with other palms, also red spider mite, so make sure the humidity is good and spray twice a day in summer.

Chamaedorea elegans Bella is one of those unfortunate plants whose name seems to alternate between this and *Neanthe bella*. *Chamaedorea* is the current favourite, but you may well find it sold as *Neanthe*. Whatever the name, it is a dwarf palm with feathery leaves, very good for home decoration. It comes from Mexico and does best in a shady place. Being slow growing, it is a good bottle garden plant (see 'Terrariums and Bottle Gardens'). Of all the palms grown in the home, it is the only one to sometimes produce flowers when it is about 60 cm (2 ft) tall—a spray of yellowish-cream-coloured tiny, round objects, looking more like a fruit than a flower.

For a description of the date palm, *Phoenix dactylifera*, see 'Plants to Grow from Pips'. *P. canariensis* is another species, growing to about 60 cm (2 ft), with a slightly bulbous stem and feathery leaves which can be 30 cm (1 ft) or more long. *Chrysalidocarpus lutescens*, the Butterfly Palm, naturally grows to 7½ m (25 ft), so it takes well to container-growing and is a good houseplant. The stems are yellowy, the leaves pinnate. The cycads are survivors from very ancient times. *Cycas revoluta* is palm-like, naturally a short plant to about 3 m (10 ft), and easily grown in warmth and humidity.

Howeia forsteriana (back), Chrysalidocarpus lutescens (centre) and Cycas revoluta (right)

Heathers

Erica gracilis✳✳✳ , E. × hyemalis✳✳✳ , E. nivalis✳✳✳

It may seem strange that varieties of heather should need to be grown in the sheltering warmth of the home, but these plants are all Cape heaths which come from South Africa, so no more need be said. The variety of heather that we are used to in Britain is a tough little plant which grows in exposed windy places, on poor soil often almost completely consisting of peat and containing a good deal of moisture. It is frequently subjected to considerable cold and attacked by a variety of animals, but in spite of this thrives and flowers profusely, from late August to October, and in winter.

Its tender cousin, the Cape heath, has some similarities apart from its general appearance; it prefers a peaty, acid soil, and likes plenty of water and a good deal of light. However, it will not stand frost, and needs to be kept reasonably warm while flowering, which it does during the winter.

These South African heaths are often given as a Christmas present—they are usually flowering at their best during December—and indeed they are very attractive. *Erica gracilis* is the one most often seen; it has a mass of small rosy purple bells all the way up spikes about 30 cm (12 in) tall. *E. x hyemalis* (the specific name is the Latin for winter) has particularly attractive small tubular blooms, deep pink tipped with white, on stumpier spikes, although the whole plant is about the same size. *E. nivalis* has white bells, and the same habit of growth as *gracilis*, of which it is probably a variety; Ville de Cherbourg is a very similar French cultivar, and *willmorei* is a very good hybrid. All have fine, needle-like leaves which, like the leaves of the Christmas tree, tend to drop when the plants are grown indoors.

Erica gracilis and *nivalis* flower naturally from September to December, so they may be coming towards the end of their flowering season if you are given them for Christmas or the New Year; *E. x hyemalis* starts to flower in December and can continue until March, depending on the plant. Some plants will be early into flower, others not until near the end of the season, but all should be in bloom for at least three weeks when they do flower.

The main difficulty when you first get the plant is to prevent it from throwing all its leaves onto the carpet at once, followed rapidly by the flowers. If you have bought it yourself, you can at least ensure that it is well protected from cold and draughts on the way home, whatever happened to it during its journey from the nursery.

It is more than likely that it will want a drink at once—if it is dry, the pot will be lightweight, and the compost surface dry and crumbly. Because the compost is mostly peat, the best method is to put the pot in a container of tepid rainwater, so that the water level comes halfway up the pot. If you have no rainwater to hand, softened water from the tap will do, but not hard water, particularly if you live in a limestone district. The water will soak up naturally like this; when the compost surface is damp, take the pot out and drain.

It is also a good idea to mist the plant, using water at room temperature, and to do this two or three times a day for a few days while the plant settles down. After that misting once a day should be enough, but it is essential to also provide humidity.

Whatever you do, don't put the plant in a draught. It will expect an even temperature of about 13°C (55°F) while it is flowering; anything which goes up during the day and down at night will cause trouble. It likes a good light and during the winter months you can stand it in early or late sunshine, not at midday. A table standing near a window is a good place.

After its initial watering, be careful not to let the plant dry out at all, as it will shed its leaves at once. Some people recommend standing it permanently in a dish of shallow water; you can try this, but watch for the opposite trouble, waterlogging. Otherwise water from the top, virtually daily, always using warm lime-free water. If you suspect that the centre of the rootball has got dry, put the entire pot in water to cover the compost surface; when bubbles of air have stopped coming up you can take the pot out, knowing that the compost is by then thoroughly wet, and let it drain.

When flowering has ended, take off the dead spikes, which will prune the plant considerably, but continue to water so that the plant can go on growing. In late March or early April, pot it on into a size larger pot, using a mixture of two-thirds fibrous peat and one-third coarse sand; liquid feed after two weeks, at about fortnightly intervals, using a potash-high fertilizer. As the new shoots grow, you can take out the tips if you like to make the plant a little bushier, but it is not essential; in any case wait for the plant to settle down in its new pot.

These heaths can be put outside for the summer, set up to the pot rim in a border where they will get the late afternoon sun. Remember to watch their water and food needs at this time. Bring them indoors as soon as the temperature starts to drop down to 7°C (45°F) at night and gradually raise the temperature to 13°C (55°F) by flowering time.

Increase of these Cape heaths is not very easy for the home grower, but if you would like to try it you can take cuttings. Use the tips of new shoots in spring, making the cuttings about 2.5 cm (1 in) long; put them in sandy peat, and keep them under plastic in a temperature near 21°C (70°F).

Erica × willmorei is a Cape Heath hybrid which flowers from winter to spring

Cyclamen ❋❋❋

Of all the beautiful plants available at Christmas for presents, the cyclamen has proved to be one of the most popular, in spite of the fact that the plants often die soon after through lack of understanding of their needs. This is such a pity; it takes about fifteen months to bring a cyclamen sown from seed to the flowering stage and, if looked after properly, it will flower for several weeks at least and can be grown for many seasons after, getting larger and larger and producing more and more flowers each year.

Today's large-flowered cyclamen comes from the small-flowered wild *Cyclamen persicum* which is found around the Eastern Mediterranean, notably Greece. The wild plant has the delicate scent of lily-of-the-valley, with white, pink or carmine flowers in various shades, appearing in late winter and spring. The leaves have silvery markings and are evergreen, which raises the question as to whether the corms of the cultivated kind should be completely dried off in summer, as is usually advised.

Cyclamen persicum derives its name from the Greek *kyklos*, circular, which refers to the way in which the seed of some species are carried. After flowering the stems are twisted round and round in a tight spiral like a spring, so that the seedheads are drawn down to the soil and the seeds can more or less sow themselves, if the mice will let them alone.

It was first introduced in 1731, and as more and more plants were grown in the greenhouses of the Victorians, so gradually larger-flowered kinds appeared, with greater variation in colour. However, the varieties that we know today seem to have appeared spontaneously, without any particular selection or breeding. At the same time the kinds with the very pretty fringed edges to the petals appeared. Unfortunately none was scented, and none had silvery markings on the leaves, but these markings have now been brought back to modern plants, and the inclusion of fragrance is once again being attempted. Colours now include salmon, magenta and light red, as well as the various pinks and carmine.

A delightful strain has been introduced recently, called the Puppet Cyclamen, which has *C. neapolitanum* as part of its parentage. Plants and flowers are very much smaller, but with fragrant flowers held well above the leaves, and with the same range of flower colour you may well prefer them to their larger relatives.

One of the reasons that makes the cyclamen difficult to keep is that it naturally flowers two months or so later than Christmas; another is that it likes cool conditions, and a third is that it should have an even temperature.

In its move from the nursery to the florist's shop, and from shop to home, it may have to put up with all sorts of temperatures, and hideous draughts. If you buy it yourself you can at least arrange that it is well wrapped while you take it home. Failure of a cyclamen is not necessarily because its new owner has maltreated it; the journey from nursery to shop to home may already have been too much for it, and no amount of attention after that will save it.

Cyclamen like coolness and humidity, unvarying temperatures and a good light, even sunlight as winter sun is hardly powerful.

While it is flowering and growing temperatures of 10–16°C (50–60°F) are ideal, with humidity supplied by moist peat or the shingle-in-a-saucer method (see page 6), and overhead misting (avoiding the flowers) every day. Central heating is useless, as is the kind of heating in which the room gets very warm during the day but then becomes almost frosty at night.

If the leaves begin to yellow, this is a sign of dry compost or alternatively waterlogged compost, too much heat or a dry atmosphere; review your watering, temperatures and humidity. Wilting leaves and flowers usually mean severe lack of water; buds falling off and stems rotting at the base can be too much water, or water lying on top of the corm. Complete collapse of the plant can indicate much too high temperatures.

You can water in one of two ways. The generally recommended method is to stand the pot in a shallow saucer of warm rainwater, leave it until no more water is being absorbed, then let it drain. The other is to water from above, which is quite safe provided about a third of the corm protrudes above the compost surface. The water can cover the surface of the compost but should not reach as high as the base of the stems. If you follow either of these methods you should not have any trouble with rotting buds and leaf stalks.

As the flowers die, remove them, complete with stems down to the corm, and when there are no more flowers to come, continue to water and feed until the leaves start their natural yellowing and dying. Then stop feeding, gradually lessen the watering, and leave the corm in its pot, quite dry, in a dark cool place until late May, when the pot can be buried to its rim in a shady border in the garden. If you have no garden, it will not matter if you leave the corm where it is until re-potting time in early August. Some growers, however, like to keep the corm ticking over gently, and keep the compost just moist so that one or two leaves are retained.

Even when the corm is left to rest completely dry, it will tell you itself when to start watering again. Incredibly, leaves will begin to appear from the surface of the corm still in the bone-dry soil, sometime in late July or early August, depending on the season, and you should repot it at once. Use a very well-drained open mixture, John Innes potting compost (see page 8) or a mix of 2 parts peat, 1 part acid loam and 1 part coarse sand. Let at least a third of the corm project above the surface, and use a larger pot if necessary—it usually is.

Water the plant normally, shade it from the sun and keep it in a temperature of about 13°–15°C (55°–60°F). Feed it fortnightly after about a month or so, and keep it free from frost; stop feeding as the flower buds begin to show and do not start again until flowering has finished.

Increase cyclamen from seed sown in a temperature of 18°C (65°F) in John Innes seed compost (see page 8) during August or September. Space the seed out singly and cover with 1 cm ($\frac{1}{2}$ in) granulated moss peat. Prick the plants out at the two to four leaf stage and pot them on as they need it, keeping them in a temperature of about 16°C (60°F) through the winter; in summer continue to grow them outdoors in the shade.

Cyclamen hybrids, specially bred to include the silvery markings on the leaves

Azaleas ✳✳✳

The Christmas-flowering azaleas are among the loveliest and most glamorous of all pot plants; a present of one of these at Christmas will ensure the popularity of the donor for at least the rest of the year! He or she will be even more popular if hints for caring for the plant are given at the same time.

First of all, a little about the history and origin of these azaleas will help in understanding their needs. They are part of the enormous group of plants called rhododendrons, from the temperate Himalayas. There they grow in woodland, where the soil is acid and contains leafmould. The pot azaleas come from *Rhododendron simsii*, the Indian azalea, a native of southern China and Indo-China. The flowers of the species are naturally variable in colour in the wild; a variety has been found with white flowers striped red, which has made the plants even more popular. The Japanese *Rh. indicum* has also been used as a source of varieties and hybrids; like *simsii*, it is evergreen, but slightly hardier, less variable in flower colour and with flowers singly or in pairs.

The colour of azaleas is in the range pink, red, salmon and all shades of these, with white included; some kinds now have stripes, or white margins to the petals, and some are frilly, or double. All are extremely free-flowering, and the plants are covered in blooms. If you handle them the right way, they will remain in flower for several weeks at least. Although deliberate hybridization has been tried, on the whole most of our modern azaleas have been produced as a result of the 'sporting' or mutation of a cluster of flowers, or a complete branch, from which cuttings have been taken.

When you receive your azalea, find out whether it needs watering or not. The clue to this is a water mark, or ring, round the main stem; the higher up this is, the less will the plant need water. If there is no mark visible at all, and if the pot feels very light and the compost surface is dry, then it will need a lot of water. The best way to soak the soil ball right through to the centre is to put the pot in a bucket of warm rainwater so that the compost surface is covered, and leave it there until bubbles stop coming up from the compost. Then take it out, put it to drain, and finally give it its rightful place of honour in the home.

If the ring is more than 1 cm ($\frac{1}{2}$ in) up the stem, on no account water the plant; it will be almost too wet. At about 1 cm ($\frac{1}{2}$ in) you can give it the normal watering, from the top of the pot. Watch the water mark whenever you are watering after this, and you shouldn't go far wrong. If the plant does get too dry it will shed its leaves at once, probably the flowers as well. Always use tepid water, free of lime. Yellow leaves, no new shoots and a thin sickly look are all signs of a limy water or compost.

The temperature while the plant is in flower should be about 16°C (60°F), but not lower than 10°C (50°F); azaleas are definitely not plants which need high temperatures, and they will suffer if you keep them in hot rooms, especially if centrally heated.

A humid atmosphere, however, is important; it is often recommended that the plants should be sprayed overhead daily, *without wetting the flowers*, but how you do this when the plant is covered in flowers, I do not know. It is probably better to mist them, to plunge the container in moist peat, or to use humidifiers. Without this they are very likely to be infested with red spider mite, or to drop their buds and leaves.

A slightly shady position is the best one; don't feed the plant while it is flowering, and remove the flowers as they die. You should also take out any new shoots which appear, until flowering has finished altogether, then let them develop naturally as it is on these shoots that the next season's flowers will appear.

There is no reason why your azalea should be thrown away as soon as flowering finishes; it is perfectly possible to keep it and flower it again the following year, if you remember that, like all other plants, it will need a resting season and a growing season beforehand.

The azalea's resting season comes in the summer, after its extension-of-shoots period, so once flowering is over cut back all the old shoots a little by about an eighth of their length to just above a side-shoot. As the new growth gets under way, repot the plant into a slightly larger pot—from 12.5 to 15 cm (5 to 6 in), for example—and use a mixture of sphagnum peat, acid-reacting leafmould and coarse sand, in equal parts, or John Innes Potting Compost No. 1 (see page 8), with added peat. Keep the plants a little warmer than 16°C (60°F)—nearer 21°C (70°F) would be better—but after two or three weeks gradually lower the temperature until the plants have been hardened sufficiently to be put out of doors in late spring, as soon as there is no further risk of frost. Keep the plants watered throughout this period.

Once out of doors, plunge the container to its rim in a bed or border where there is dappled shade—too heavy shade will prevent flower buds developing later. Give liquid feed once every two weeks, and in very hot weather mist occasionally with lime-free water. This is their ripening period, during which watering should not be neglected.

In September, or before the time when frosts are due, lift the containers and take the plants back indoors, put them in the usual light but not sunny position, stop feeding, and water sparingly. With temperatures slightly higher than they were outdoors, buds will develop more quickly; as they begin to appear, increase the quantity of water. The flower buds will be round and plump, and you should have the plant in flower again soon after Christmas, if not actually then.

The plants will grow very large if you are successful, needing containers of 30- and 37-cm (12- and 14-in) diameter as they grow older. A wide shallow container is best as they are inclined to be surface-rooting. You can increase azaleas by taking cuttings of young shoots in summer, and growing them with bottom heat.

Azaleas come in all shades of red, crimson and rose-pink, more than welcome during the winter

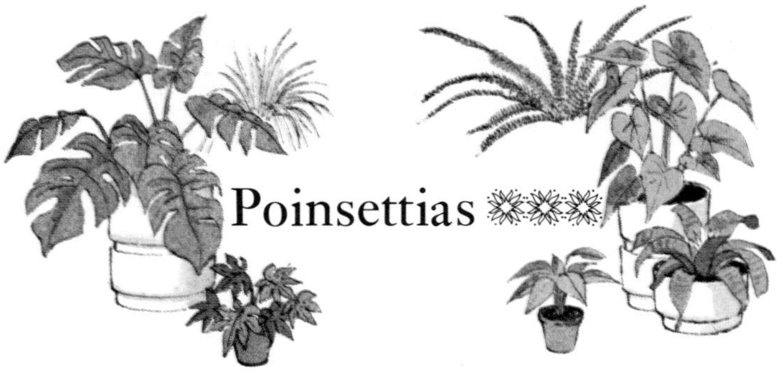

Poinsettias

The 'pretty euphorbia' is a literal translation of the botanical name of the poinsettia, and there could not be a better way of describing it. *Euphorbia pulcherrima* was found in the early nineteenth century by a Dr Poinsett in Mexico, where it is a deciduous shrub or small tree of about 3 m (10 ft) tall.

The euphorbia plant family is an extraordinarily mixed collection of plants. Many of them are the kind cultivated in gardens or seen as weeds, with yellowish-green leaves, called spurges; the plant called the Crown of Thorns is *E. splendens*, an extremely spiny specimen. There are some from Cape Province which look exactly like cacti, and there is *E. fulgens*, sold as a cut flower by florists, which is a shrub with slender branches, willow-like leaves and wreaths of small, bright orange-red flowers. The one thing they all have in common, besides the same kind of flowers, is the milky sap which oozes out when the branches or stems are injured or cut. In some species this is poisonous, but not in the poinsettia.

The bright scarlet 'petals' of the poinsettia are not real flowers; they are the bracts, and the flowers, tiny and yellow, are inside them. The change in the form of the plant from a comparatively large individual of 3 m (10 ft) to a pot plant of about 45–60 cm ($1\frac{1}{2}$–2 ft) with a mass of flowers on top is something of a triumph for the breeders and growers. They have first had to reduce the size, then to make the plant flower a good deal earlier than it does normally, and finally to ensure that it does not shed its leaves as soon as it is taken out of nursery conditions.

Fortunately poinsettias root easily from cuttings, and by taking these at the right time quite small bushy plants were produced, but not with very good flowers. Extra heat and adjustment of the day length improved their size and colour, but leaf-dropping was a problem. Eventually an American grower called Mikkelsen was able to produce a much hardier race of plants which would put up with changes in temperature, and which would survive temperatures lower than normal. Two very well-known varieties now grown are Ecke Pink and Eckespoint, both called after their breeder Paul Ecke.

The modern poinsettia is now a beautiful, easily grown pot plant, which can be kept and grown on for several years. Unfortunately, one still sees unhappy plants consisting of bare poles with a red tuft on top, usually because their owner has forgotten that they are living, and that they need water and warmth.

So much work has gone into the breeding and selection of the poinsettia to produce an attractive and manageable plant that, if only for the sake of your conscience, you should do your best for it. Remember, as always, that the plant was originally growing in ideal nursery conditions, and that since then it has been kept in a shop and has put up with several journeys, so it is best given four-star treatment to start with, a really even temperature of about 18°C (65°F), plenty of humidity, and a little shade (it may, even so, lose one or two leaves).

Once the plant has settled down, then the temperature can vary a little; it does not matter if it drops slightly below 16°C (60°F) at night, and the light can vary between bright and slightly shaded. Misting daily is a necessity, and a humidifier would be ideal, but failing that, a wide shallow plate with shingle and water in it is a good second best.

Poinsettias do not drink a great deal when in flower but it is advisable to have a look at the compost every day. Use tepid water but do make sure first that the plant really needs it. Over-watering will make the leaves drop as quickly as cold, a dry atmosphere or drought. If in doubt, keep the plant slightly on the dry side, but mist the leaves regularly. If they begin to wilt, then water is needed at the roots. Don't subject your poinsettia to gas or draughts.

After several weeks, the leaves will naturally begin to turn yellow and the flowers will die; they can be cut off, removing the flowerhead but not the leaves. Gradually decrease watering until the compost is barely moist, and rest the plant for two or three months. Then give it a heavy watering, cut the stems back to about 10 cm (4 in), and put it in a warm sunny place, on a window-sill or in a greenhouse. Dust the cut stems with charcoal or cigarette ash to stop the flow of white sap.

New shoots will appear from the remains of the stems and you can then do one of two things. First, the plants can be repotted, using completely fresh John Innes Potting Compost No. 1 (see page 8) and potting into small 8-cm ($3\frac{1}{2}$-in) pots. Water only a little until the shoots really get going, and later pot on into 12.5-cm (5-in) pots when the roots have filled the smaller pots, and in successive years into 20-cm (8-in) pots.

The other method is to take cuttings from the new shoots when they are 7.5–10 cm (3–4 in) long, and this is probably better as it will give you new and more vigorous plants. Stop the 'bleeding' as described, and put the cuttings in a mixture of equal parts of coarse sand and peat, covered by a plastic bag, with a temperature of about 21°C (70°F). Then pot on the rooted cuttings as they require it in the John Innes potting composts (see page 8), give them a good light, but not summer sun, and a temperature of at least 16°C (60°F). Feed at two- to three-week intervals, from early August, but stop feeding when the flowers begin to form. Stem lengthening and leaf development will have ended some months before this.

Poinsettias are what is called 'short-day' plants, that is, they will only develop flower buds when the days are shorter than the nights. So they must be kept in a room which has natural day length in autumn and early winter—no artificial light during the naturally dark hours between October and the end of December. This applies whether you have taken cuttings or are growing on the old plant.

A variety of poinsettia called Mikkelrochford, treated with a dwarfing chemical

Aphelandra and *Pachystachys*

Aphelandra squarrosa Louisae (Zebra Plant)✳✳✳,
Pachystachys lutea✳✳

The aphelandra is a striking, rather bushy plant; its bright, deep yellow flowerheads and white-patterned leaves ensure that it is attractive both in and out of flower for many weeks in winter. It is a member of the plant family called the *Acanthaceae*, and it was the leaf of another member of the same family, the *Acanthus*, which was used as a model for the decoration of the top of Corinthian columns. Pachystachys belongs to the same family, but its leaves are plain green and the deep yellow flower spike is much longer.

The Zebra Plant—its leaves provide the reason for the common name—comes from Brazil and was introduced in 1800. With modern methods of propagation, and care, it was found to be suitable for growing in the home, and it need no longer be confined to a warm greenhouse. Like a good many other house plants, it has gradually become hardier over the years. Cuttings were taken from the strongest and fittest plants, and these were the ones that could stand up the best to less natural conditions; each generation adapted itself slightly further. A plant straight from the tropics, and the same species grown here from cuttings over many years, are likely to need quite different treatment.

Aphelandra grows to about 60–90 cm (2–3 ft). It can be bought in flower any time between November and January. As a Christmas gift it will need extra care, as do the cyclamen, azalea and poinsettia and, like them, it would be a pity for such a handsome and expensive plant to lose its leaves and then its flowers for lack of a little understanding.

Dry atmospheres and lack of water at the roots are the main causes of leaf drop; do keep the leaves misted daily, with tepid water, and supply a humid atmosphere by standing the container on shingle in a shallow dish of water. You will probably find that the plant wants watering every day, depending on the temperature, as it drinks a great deal while in flower, and the leaves will immediately show even slight dryness by wilting. Give it a good watering, let the extra water drain out and then look at the plant again the next day; you should always use tepid water.

The tubular yellow flowers shoot out from between the deeper yellow bracts at intervals for about three weeks, but when they have finished the bracts gradually lose their yellowness and the whole flowerhead should be cut off, back to the first pair of leaves. This should be done to all the flowers, whether the main head or from sideshoots. The leaves will last for some weeks more, though you may lose one or two at the base, and while they are still green and healthy you can continue feeding and watering.

In February, however, the plant should be allowed to rest and gradually dried off until the compost is barely moist. In early April, it will need cutting back to about 5 cm (2 in); give it fresh John Innes potting compost (see page 8), and probably a larger pot, though these plants flower best if potbound. You can also use a compost mixture of equal parts by volume of loam, sand and leafmould or peat, with half a teaspoonful of general fertilizer mixed into each 12-cm (5-in) potful.

The temperature while the plant is growing and flowering should be about 16–21°C (60–70°F), but lower while it is resting, about 10°C (50°F).

When the aphelandra is started into growth again, raise the temperature and water normally after repotting and pruning. Sideshoots will come from the stumps of the old plant, and possibly from below the soil; you can let these grow on steadily, taking out the tips once or twice to make the plant bushy. Give it a good light, even sunlight, provided it is not summer or midday sun, and start to liquid feed when the flower buds can first be seen. Continue to feed until flowering finishes, using a fertilizer with a high potash content. You may find that flowering starts earlier than the previous season.

Increase of these plants is by cuttings, using the tops of sideshoots produced after the flowerheads are removed. Rooting the cuttings is not very easy unless you can heat the compost in which they are being struck. The compost, by the way, should be well-drained and sandy.

It is only recently that *Pachystachys lutea* has been introduced as an indoor plant; before that the only species of the genus known and grown in cultivation was *P. coccinea*, a shrubby plant with bright red flowerheads 15 cm (6 in) long. The name is formed directly from two Greek words, meaning 'thick' and 'spike', respectively; the flowers are densely packed in a long, rather than round, flowerhead. It has bright, deep yellow bracts and white flowers. The leaves are plain green.

The home of the pachystachys genus is the West Indies and tropical America, but *lutea* will stand the same kind of temperatures as aphelandra. It can, in fact, be treated in more or less the same way, although flowering may be in autumn or winter and it can even be had in flower in late spring. It is slightly less temperamental than aphelandra, and will accept slightly lower temperatures while it is resting. Neither plant seems to be bothered by gas, but draughts will upset them both badly.

Aphelandra squarrosa Louisae is ornamental even when out of flower

African violets

Saintpaulia ionantha ✽✽✽

The African violet is named after its discoverer, Baron Saint-paul-Illaire, who introduced it in 1893. It really is an African plant, from Tanzania in East Africa, and can be found as far up the mountains as 1,000 m (3,000 ft) above sea level. However, in East Africa it is still warm even at that height, and very humid.

The saintpaulia is a lovely plant to grow indoors; the purple flowers produced in such quantities for so long during the year put it among the top ten. It would be the top of the ten if it were an easier plant to grow, but unfortunately African violets either grow and flower tremendously, or fade away and get smaller and smaller, until they are not worth keeping. Healthy growth seems to depend particularly on a good light and an even temperature.

The species saintpaulia naturally produces purple flowers, but since its introduction it has been the subject of a good deal of selection and hydridization, and there is now quite a wide colour range of shades of violet, almost blue, plum, pink and white. There are some blue-violet kinds with white edges to the petals and other varieties with double flowers, frilly petals, or leaves varying between light and dark green, smooth or hairy. For me, they would be perfect if only they had fragrance.

The early hybrids and varieties tended to drop their flowers as soon as they died on to the leaves below, which resulted in rotting, but strains have now been produced which hold their flowers. The Diana strain of saintpaulia is a particularly good one, with non-dropping flowers—it was developed by the German nurseryman Englert. These saintpaulias are not usually sold by name, but if you do come across some labelled kinds, Pink Cloud (double), Flying Dutchman (purple-blue), Silver Lining (double blue frilly, white picotee edge) and White Rhapsody (double) are particularly reliable and good. If you like plants with variegated leaves, there are one or two of these amongst the saintpaulias, with creamy markings on the green.

As with any plant, it is better to go with Nature than against it, and it helps to know when the natural flowering season of the saintpaulia occurs. The unfortunate owner can be forgiven for not knowing, since the plants can flower several times during the year, but usually they will start to show buds in July, and finish flowering about the following February or March. In the mean-time they will have flowered continuously, but with several greater bursts of flowers every two months or so. They will need to rest between March and mid-May.

You will more than likely buy or be given your saintpaulia while it is in flower; provided you remember that it will not need to rest after the current flower flush has spent itself, unless the time is late February, you should be able to keep it healthy without difficulty if you give it the following care.

It has been said that saintpaulias take in almost more moisture through their leaves than they do through their roots, so you can see that humidity is vital. It is best to stand them in a wide shallow dish of water and shingle permanently, so that water is constantly evaporating up round them. Another good tactic which they enjoy is the occasional steam bath; put the pot in a bowl, put this bowl in a much larger one and pour boiling water into the larger bowl—the steam seems to do the plants a power of good.

Temperature is important; a steady 16°C (60°F) will do the most good, but you can let it go up and down in the range 21°C (70°F)–13°C (55°F) between day and night, provided it goes no lower. The higher the temperature, the greater the need for humidity. Whatever else you do, don't put your saintpaulia in a draught.

Light also seems to have a great effect on a saintpaulia; not enough results in few or no flowers. You can stand it in the sun during autumn and winter, but not in strong summer sunlight, although it will still need a good indirect light. If it refuses to flower, try putting it in a different place, or stand it near to a shaded lamp at night (too much light will bleach the leaves).

Watering, as always, should be done with care. Use water at room temperature and keep it off the leaves, otherwise they will develop white marks, and away from the crown which will rot if it gets wet. Saintpaulias do not need a great deal of water and their fine roots will easily be swamped—it is best to water only when the compost surface is dry. Keeping the plant on the dry side will encourage flowering.

Little feeding is required; perhaps every three weeks, with a potash-high fertilizer, during the autumn and winter.

In late winter, when your plant ceases to flower and does not produce any new leaves, it is going into its resting period, and will look fairly unhappy for two months or so. It should not be fed, only watered occasionally and given less light, until one day you suddenly find that a new leaf is coming. You can then repot it into moist peaty compost (such as 3 parts peat, 1 loam and 1 coarse sand). Plastic pots or clay pots can be used; you can also try pans as the plants are shallow-rooting. Keep the pots on the small side—10 cm (5 in) in diameter is ample for a big plant and 8 cm (3½ in) will often be large enough. There is no need to repot your saintpaulia every year, providing you have been feeding it; every two or three years is probably sufficient.

African violets are easily increased from leaf cuttings, especially if you can keep the compost warm as well as the air. Take off a good healthy leaf in January or February, with the stalk attached, put it in a rooting compost to a depth of 1 cm (½ in) and enclose in a plastic bag. After about three weeks, tiny leaves should appear at the base of the parent leaf stalk and there may be one or more new baby plants. Each of these can be detached with roots, and potted separately. If you can bear to, take off the first flowers when they appear, for better long-term results.

See also 'All-Year-Round Plants'.

The African violets are very popular house plants, with hundreds of varieties

Pelargoniums

Geraniums of all kinds are popular in gardens and homes everywhere, a sure indication of their indestructibility—of all the plants grown in pots the geranium has a unique vitality and life force which seems to be unquenchable.

The pelargoniums as a whole are native to South Africa and are used to very hot and very dry conditions, and not very much food, though the environment is not as severe as that in which cacti live. In their native land they can be seen trained over the whole of one side of a house, covered in flowers. The parents of modern hybrids and varieties were mostly introduced during the eighteenth century as a result of the explorations of a Scottish plant-hunter called Francis Masson, from Kew Botanical Gardens. He was responsible for sending back to England a great number of the plants which are now grown in greenhouses, and consequently in our homes.

Pelargoniums are particularly suitable for growing on sunny windowsills; they are flowering plants which will literally give a sheet of dazzling colour during summer. The zonal pelargoniums (geraniums) can start to flower in June and yet still be producing fresh flower clusters in November. They have rounded heads, about 10 or 12.5 cm (4 or 5 in) wide, of comparatively small flowers coloured red, salmon, pink, white, magenta or crimson, and they may be single or double. If you are doubtful as to whether you have a geranium (a zonal pelargonium) or a regal pelargonium, you can tell by the leaves; the geraniums are known as zonal because of a dark-coloured band round the leaf on the upper surface. In addition the geraniums have smallish flowers, quite a lot in one cluster, whereas the regals have large, single, trumpet-like and sometimes frilly flowers, very pretty and worthy of another name sometimes given them: the French geranium.

There are a great number of named varieties of geranium, for instance, Orangesonne, orange-salmon; Charles Gounod, white and magenta; King of Denmark, salmon; Paul Crampel, vermilion; Maxim Kovaleski, orange; Eric Lee, magenta; and, of course, the bright scarlet Gustav Emich.

The Regals usually have only one flowering period during July and early August, but if you can give them a really light position during winter, a suitable temperature and choose the right varieties, they will flower in winter also. Watch for whitefly, which apparently regard them in the same way as greenfly do cinerarias. Amongst the many hybrids in circulation, the following are good: Carisbrooke, pale pink with magenta blotches; Grand Slam, red; Aztec, white, strawberry and brown; Chiquita, rose red; Georgia Peach, frilled peach pink; Lavender Slam; White Chiffon; and Grandma Fischer, salmon-orange. All these except Carisbrooke and Chiquita will be suitable for flowering in winter.

If miniature plants attract you, there are plenty of miniature hybrids amongst the geraniums (in the region of 300!), for instance, Chi Chi, peach pink; Fleurette, deep pink; Red Admiral; and Sunstar, orange.

It is nice to have a plant or two of the scented-leaved species to finger occasionally for the pungent fragrance given off by the leaves; their flowers are tiny, but one or two have ornamental leaves, such as *P. crispum variegatum*, which is lemon-scented, with tiny curled leaves edged with yellow, and *P. quercifolium*, strongly aromatic and with almost fern-like leaves.

The coloured-leaved kind are zonals, which not only have the dark band but also other colours: Mrs H. Cox, yellow, red, brown and green leaves, salmon-pink flowers; Bronze Corinne, yellow leaf with bronze zone, red flowers; Happy Thought, yellow or white markings on green, crimson flowers; and Crocodile, prominent white veins on a green background.

Finally there are the trailing ivy-leaved kind; L'Elegante is very attractive, with a mass of small white flowers poised above trailing stems decorated with ivy-shaped leaves, edged with white, which flushes pink if the plant is kept on the dry side.

If you use a little cunning in growing your pelargoniums you can have them in flower in the winter as well as all summer; it is a matter of knowing the right time to root cuttings, and of applying a suitable environment in winter.

For general care of these plants, use John Innes Potting Compost No. 2 (see page 8), and on no account forget to put pieces of broken pot at the bottom of the container. They undoubtedly do best in 12.5-cm (5-in) clay pots—the plastic ones do not produce as good results—and, if fed at all, should be given weak doses of a potash-high fertilizer every one or two weeks to encourage further flowers. Liquid feeding, however, is often not necessary. Give them sun and warmth while they are growing, and do *not* overdo the water; you can let them get quite dry without harm, but if they do have rather a long gap between waterings, plunge them in a bucket to moisten the rootball thoroughly. Humidity is not necessary. Remove the flowers when they are finished.

From autumn onwards, gradually give less water, and keep the plants nearly completely dry until early spring; then cut them back hard, to leave about 10-cm (4-in)-long stems, and repot when growth is well started. This is the treatment for zonals, ivy-leaved, scented and coloured-leaved kinds. The Regals should be allowed to rest and dry out a little after flowering, then in late summer repot them into fresh John Innes Potting Compost No. 2, and cut them back hard. Keep them at about 7°C (45°F) and just moist until January, then increase the watering and temperature to 10–13°C (50–55°F); flowering should start again in spring.

Cuttings of all kinds should be taken in late summer, using 7.5-cm (3-in) tips of new shoots (without flowerbuds) between late July and early August. Put the cuttings into peat, vermiculite, sand, loam or mixtures of any of these; once rooted they can be transferred to 7.5-cm (3-in) pots of John Innes Potting Compost No. 1 and kept in these through the winter, with little water and low temperatures. In spring they can be increased and the young plants then transferred, as they fill their pots with roots, to 12.5-cm (5-in) pots; stop them once or twice to increase future flowering.

For winter-flowering plants, take cuttings in spring and remove all potential flower buds from the rooted plants until the end of September. Pot on as for summer-rooted cuttings, and give them as much light as possible and a temperature of 10–13°C (50–55°F) through the winter. Flowering should start about the beginning of November, but it will be determined by the time disbudding ended; flowers will come a few weeks later.

The Regal pelargonium Mrs E. Hickman

Terrariums

Growing plants in the home is an absorbing and decorative hobby. With the extra warmth of today's homes, the range of plants which can be kept has been considerably extended. There is always a reverse side to the coin, however, and with extra warmth often comes dry air, which is bad for plants and humans alike.

You can overcome this problem by growing the plants inside closed glass containers; the plants maintain the necessary humidity themselves by giving off water vapour, which is trapped in the container, condenses on the sides and runs down into the compost, to be absorbed by the roots. The bottle or glass garden maintains itself and has its own life cycle—it needs very little care once planted, and is highly ornamental.

The conventional bottle garden is the kind in which a carboy is used, either 22.5 or 45 litre (5 or 10 gallon), with a balloon-shaped body and a very narrow mouth, making planting an operation for the precise and delicate-fingered. In recent years, however, the scope has widened to include glass containers of all shapes and sizes, provided the glass is clear and they can be closed in some way: sweet jars, wine jars, hanging plastic or glass bubbles, square or rectangular cases (like the Wardian cases used by the Victorians), chemist's jars, Victorian domes, goldfish bowls and even large brandy glasses. One of the latest decorative ideas is glass coffee tables, with the plants contained between two layers of glass.

The plants you will be growing in these containers should be chosen according to their rate of growth and final size, bearing in mind also the size of the container you are going to use. There are plenty of plants which do not grow very tall, and some which can be used for ground cover. All the plants will be grown for their decorative leaves, not their flowers—the light in these glass containers is obviously decreased and if plants are to flower they must have plenty of light, so flowering plants are out unless you are using a wide-mouthed container, when you can try spring-flowering bulbs. But somehow a true bottle garden implies a collection of leafy plants, giving a rather jungly effect, green and shadowed and mysterious. The humidity and warmth inherent in such containers are highly suitable for plants which flourish in jungle conditions, but obviously not for flowers which naturally grow in light surroundings.

Some suggestions for bottle garden plants are the Starfish bromeliads (*Cryptanthus*), the palms *Chamaedorea elegans* and *Syagrus weddelliana*, *Peperomia caperata*, ferns such as *Asplenium nidus* and *Pteris cretica* Albo-lineata, marantas, *Fittonia verschaffeltii argyroneura*, *Helxine soleirolii* (Baby's Tears), *Pilea cadierei*, small-leaved ivies, *Ficus pumila* and small dracaenas. This is just to give you an idea—there are plenty more.

Whatever plants you use, they should be quite tiny to start with, from a 5-cm (2-in) pot, and about five to nine plants will probably be enough for a carboy, depending of course on its size.

Remember that the plants are all going to grow and increase in spread and height, so they need to be planted with space between them. Try to contrast the type of leaf and leaf colours, and the habit of growth, to get as much visual interest into the container as possible. The glass will enhance the appearance of the miniature garden considerably, but it will also show up mistakes in arrangement.

When planting a bottle garden, you will need the following ingredients and tools: compost, gravel or some other kind of drainage material, small plants, water, a long stiff paper funnel which will reach to the bottom of the container, an ordinary kitchen fork, a spoon, a strong wire hook or a pair of long-handled sugar tongs, a cotton reel, a small sponge, a child's paintbrush and a razor blade. The tools should be bound to canes of suitable length for manipulating inside the container.

It is a good idea, before you begin planting, to assemble all your plants on a piece of paper the same size and shape as the base of the container, in the pattern in which you would like to plant them. You will then be able to see whether your choice fits well together, and you will avoid a muddled planting when you do begin. By the way, put in those plants first which will be nearest to the glass, and finish with the central ones.

Drainage material should go in first, either gravel, shingle, pieces of broken clay pot or pebbles, in a layer about 3–5 cm (1–2 in) thick, through the paper funnel. Then the compost the same way; this can consist of 2 parts John Innes Potting Compost No. 1 (see page 8) and 1 part peat. The compost is better if sterilized; you don't want strange seeds sprouting or fungus diseases infecting the plant roots, to say nothing of the possibility of dormant insects coming to life.

The mixture should be moist and crumbly, poured in to a depth of 5–10 cm (2–4 in), or even more, depending on the container size. Tamp it down fairly firmly with the cotton reel, and then, using the spoon, make the first hole at the side of the container.

Now comes the most fiddly job, if you are using a carboy: the actual planting. Take a plant, knock most of the the soil off its roots, hold it either in the tongs or on the hooked wire and gently insert it through the opening and into the hole in the compost. Hold it in position and spread its roots out with the fork, then draw compost over them, again with the fork, and use the cotton reel for firming, making sure that the plant is upright. It is important that it is as well firmed as possible.

Continue with each plant, working towards the centre. When you have finished, pour in about half a cupful of water slowly through a funnel or a long-spouted watering can, directing it down the sides, which will also help to clean them. Brush any soil off the plants with the paintbrush, and if still necessary, clean the container inside with the sponge.

Put the finished bottle garden in a slightly shaded warm place, and insert the stopper. Condensation is likely to form after a few days, but provided there is only a little near the top of the container, you can leave the stopper on. If the condensation is so considerable that you cannot see the plants, take the stopper out for a day or two. No condensation at all means a little more water is needed. Once you have adjusted the moisture content correctly, you need not water again for several months, and even then only a small quantity will be required.

Bottle gardens, or terrariums, provide a miniature ornamental greenhouse for plants in the home

Bonsai ✻✻✻

Miniature trees which are perfect copies of giant forest trees have been grown by the Japanese under the name bonsai for at least 800 years. Bonsai is an art which was first practised by the Chinese and it is in fact a Chinese word; it means literally 'planted in a shallow dish', but its modern interpretation is 'artificially dwarfed tree'.

There are some trees still growing which are 500 years old, and not a few mere youngsters of 40 or 50 years which have become family heirlooms. Bonsai takes its place in the Japanese philosophy, and the small trees become objects of worship; they have a special place in Japanese homes and are treated with reverence, in the same way that Japanese floral art is also associated with their religion and philosophy.

The art of bonsai originally started because someone, probably an enthusiastic gardener, came across stunted specimens of this type of tree clinging to windswept cliffs and rocks on mountain tops, and was sufficiently intrigued by the shapes chiselled out by constant wind, allied to lack of food and water, to lift them and continue the process. From this it was a short step to growing them from scratch which, moreover, allowed complete control over the final shape and habit of growth.

These tiny trees have tremendous charm and fascination and, as you will find, if you start growing your own from seedlings, they are not difficult to train.

What kind of trees can you grow as bonsai? Most of the conifers, that is the evergreen, needle-bearing trees, such as the pines, spruces, firs, junipers and cypresses, and also larch which is not evergreen but is needle-bearing, respond very well and look centuries old in a matter of a few years, if treated correctly. Some of the broad-leaved trees which drop their leaves in winter can also be grown, for instance, beech, Japanese acers, crabapple, oak, birch, ginkgo, willow, rowan and elm, as well as shrubs such as japonica, cotoneaster, pyracantha, and even the climbing wisteria.

These trees are all hardy and in fact they must have cool conditions outdoors in winter when they are dormant. But you can also grow some of the more tender plants as bonsai, for instance, *Ficus diversifolia*, *F. benjamina*, *Pittosporum tobira* and the citrus species (lemon, orange, etc), and there is no reason why you should not experiment with other slightly tender house plants of a tree or shrub nature, using those which are reasonably slow-growing.

One sometimes sees a bonsai grotesquely stunted and shaped; this is not really the aim. You should try to obtain a perfectly proportioned small tree, with its top growth and main trunk in balance—you should have the impression that you are looking at a normally sized, fully grown tree through the wrong end of a telescope.

Sometimes the poor shape is because the bonsai has been grafted by the nurseryman in an attempt to hurry up Nature in order to sell the specimen quickly—growing true bonsai is not the way to a swift fortune. You can usually pick these out, however; the graft is out of proportion to the rest of the tree, and at an awkward angle, and the bonsai often has the top obviously cut off when the tree was some years old, rather than pinched out at the seedling stage.

Probably the most satisfying way to grow a bonsai is to start with a seed or seedling; you can control its growth completely then, and shape it exactly as you like. Sow the seed in a proprietary seed compost in early spring, putting one seed in a 5-cm (2-in) container—a clay pot or even a yoghurt carton with drainage holes punched in the bottom is suitable. Keep it watered and in a good light. There is no need to provide heat for germination, unless you are using slightly tender plants, but the seed may be slow to sprout, so be patient; sometimes it will take a year before seed leaves appear.

When the seedling is growing well, and a root or roots are just appearing through the drainage holes, it can be given its first root pruning, using nail scissors. Take the seedling out of the container and remove most of the compost from the roots to see what type of root you are dealing with. The thick tap or anchoring roots can be cut back almost completely; finer roots are cut back only a little.

Then repot the seedling firmly in the same pot and fresh compost, and repeat the root pruning process, if necessary, towards the end of the growing season. What you are aiming at is as many fibrous roots, the feeders, as possible.

At the same time as you prune the roots, you should check the top growth by pinching back the tips of the side shoots, or by removing those which are too strong-growing and which would ultimately throw the tree out of balance. The tip of the leading shoot should be removed only when the main stem has reached the length required for the mature tree; this may be in the first or second season.

In the second season, root and shoot pruning will again be required in the same way, continuing with the same container and new compost at each pruning. In the third spring the tree can be put in its permanent container, most suitable if it is one of the square, rectangular or rounded shallow pots, glazed or unglazed, used by the Japanese.

Prune the roots again when you are lifting the tree, and, if the growth is to be trained forward, set it in the centre or slightly towards the back of the container. If it is top-heavy, weigh the roots down with a stone or two, or train them over the stones so that they are partly out of the compost (this gives an authentic aged effect later on) and pass string over the top and under the container temporarily until the roots have taken hold of the stone.

Further root-pruning will be needed every year in late spring, but not a hard one, only a gentle trim. The top growth will also need stopping and, very important, training. Pruning will do this to some extent, by removing badly placed shoots, or too strong ones. You should have a good idea in your mind's eye, as each seedling develops, of the kind of shape you want the mature tree to be; as well as pruning, tying or weighing the shoots down with stones will persuade them to grow in the right direction. Wiring, with copper or plastic-coated wire, will also help give the desired moulding of the tree. Keep an eye on the wire so that you can remove it before it cuts the bark.

Bonsai need cool temperatures, a good light, watering most days while they are growing, and a weak liquid feed every two weeks or so. Hardy specimens can spend alternate weeks in the growing season outdoors, but while dormant they should be continuously outdoors.

A good example of Bonsai: a miniature juniper

Indoor bulbs

Clivia miniata (Kafir Lily)✳✳ , Hippeastrum (Amaryllis)✳✳ ,
Vallota speciosa (Scarborough Lily)✳✳

This group of bulbs has particularly beautiful, large, lily-like flowers. All have been crossed amongst their own species to produce hybrids in a great variety of colours and it is possible to have the Kafir Lily, the amaryllis and the Scarborough Lily all flowering one after the other. Sometimes there is difficulty in getting the bulbs to flower; this is usually due to insufficient food or the wrong kind of food, or to insufficient ripening.

The Kafir Lily comes from Natal, in South Africa, and was named after one of the Duchesses of Northumberland, of the Clive family. It is the only one of the three which is evergreen, and even when resting its glossy, strap-shaped leaves do not die down. Clusters of at least twelve orange flowers in a single head, each nearly 7.5 cm (3 in) long and with yellow centres, burst into bloom in early spring and last for several weeks. As the plants get older, they will produce more and more flowers. Red berries follow the flowers, and the seeds of these will germinate quite easily to produce flowering-sized bulbs about four years later, provided they are kept growing all the time and are never dried off. The height of the flower stems is about 45 cm (1½ ft).

When the Kafir Lily is in flower it does best in moderate warmth, about 16°C (60°F), particularly a steady warmth; it will grow in a little shade, a good light or some sun—it is not choosy, provided the light conditions are not extreme either way. After flowering continue to water plentifully, as the plant will produce new leaves during the summer, and keep it at about the same temperature; liquid feed once a week with a potash-high fertilizer. Kafir Lilies will put up with a dry atmosphere, but no plant except cacti really likes it, and besides humidity, the occasional bath with overhead spraying will be appreciated.

In autumn, watering should gradually be reduced from October onwards until the compost is kept only just moist; no feeding will be required during the winter, and the temperature can be lowered to 4–7°C (40–45°F). The plant must have a proper rest at this time, otherwise it will not flower again. In February the temperature can be raised and more water given, and when the flower stem is about 15 cm (6 in) tall feeding can start again. If you increase the water and warmth earlier than February, flowering will also start earlier.

Clivia will gradually fill the pot with its fleshy roots, and it should then be repotted in February, just as growth is about to start again, using John Innes Potting Compost No. 1 (see page 8). You can also increase the plants at the same time, by dividing the roots, but they are usually very entangled and you must be prepared for some injury and the necessity of throwing part of the plant away. Pot up into 12.5–25-cm (5–10-in) pots; clivias flower better if slightly potbound, so do not use too large a pot.

The hippeastrum, commonly known as amaryllis, is an exceedingly showy plant, with large trumpet-shaped flowers, sometimes as much as 15 or 17 cm (6 or 7 in) wide, and two, three or four on one stem. Colours vary between brilliant scarlet, pink, white, crimson and all shades of these, some spotted on a white background, others edged with a darker colour. Some especially beautiful hybrids are Apple Blossom, pale pink with a white

throat; Belinda, deep velvety red; Fiery Diamond, an intense glowing orange-red; Mont Blanc, pure white except for a pale green throat; and Picotee, white with red freckles and a red edge to the petals—the throat is light green. There are many more stocked by specialist bulb nurserymen, but if you are a beginner with hippeastrums you can buy perfectly good unnamed ones.

Flowering time can start in December, if you buy prepared bulbs, but in general the bulbs will flower in succession according to variety and treatment from February to April. Bulbs are available from mid- to late winter. Half fill a pot about 2.5 cm (1 in) wider than the bulb with John Innes Potting Compost No. 2 (see page 8), forming it into a cone so that the bulb can sit on top. Then fill in compost round the bulb so that it is half buried, leaving a 2-cm (¾-in) or so space at the top for watering. Give a good watering, put the pot in a place where there is heat coming up from underneath and semi-shade, and leave it alone. When the leaves begin to lengthen, by which time the flower stem should also be appearing, water normally and put it in a lighter place. Too much water too early produces leaves at the expense of the flowers. When the flower stem is about 30 cm (1 ft) tall, put the plant in a sunny place.

Once the flowers have finished, cut the flower stem off completely, and start feeding every week; hippeastrum needs as much warmth and sun as possible at this time until growth slows down at the end of July. Watering should then gradually be decreased and feeding should stop. From then until October the plants ripen and will still need as much heat and sun as possible; then they can be dried off completely or kept very slightly moist. The temperature in winter should not fall below 10°C (50°F). Leave the plants alone until signs of growth begin to appear, then give them a good watering and start the cycle again.

Topdress by removing the top 2 cm (¾-in) or so of soil and replacing it with new compost every year as growth is starting; complete repotting will only be necessary every four years or so. Increase by offsets removed when you are repotting.

Vallota speciosa, the Scarborough Lily, grows wild in South Africa, and flowers in late summer and early autumn, in a beautiful shade of red. It is altogether a smaller plant than hippeastrum, with two or three funnel-shaped flowers about 10 cm (4 in) long on each 30-cm (12-in) stem. It is rather easier to grow and flower than hippeastrum, bulbs being potted in spring or summer. Use John Innes Potting Compost No. 2 (see page 8), and put three bulbs in a 17-cm (7-in) pot, almost completely burying them. Give them a little water and put them in a sunny place with a temperature of 10°C (50°F) until they begin to grow in earnest. Then water rather more and, when the flowers have finished and have been removed, water freely until the leaves begin to die; then gradually dry off and rest through spring and early summer. Always give them as much light as possible—a window position is ideal. Leave them undisturbed until the pot is really crowded, as they flower much better when left alone, and after the first year feed during the growing season, but only about once a month. Too much food at this time will result in offset production rather than flowers.

See also 'Autumn-flowering Plants'.

A striking example of the beautiful flowers of the hippeastrum, or amaryllis

Miniature indoor bulbs

Chionodoxa luciliae (Glory of the Snow)＊, Crocus＊, *Galanthus nivalis* (Snowdrop)＊, Freesia＊, *Iris reticulata*＊, *Muscari azureum* (Grape Hyacinth)＊, Narcissus (Daffodil)＊, *Scilla sibirica*＊

Flowers for winter and early spring are always welcome. All these bulbs flower naturally at this time of year, but by growing them indoors they will bloom a week or ten days earlier than normal, though they cannot be hurried on as much as the forced or prepared bulbs. Except for the freesias, none grow more than about 15 cm (6 in) tall. The iris, grape hyacinths, some of the narcissi and the freesias are fragrant.

The Glory of the Snow produces single flowers in late February, in different shades of blue, according to variety, on 10–15-cm (4–6-in) stems; there is now a pink-flowered variety called Pink Giant.

Crocus come in all sorts of different shades of yellow and purple, also white and almost blue, purple-feathered white, yellow-shaded bronze, cream and so on. There is a much greater range of colours than most people realize, and it pays to order them from a bulb specialist who stocks a wide range. They will flower from early February to April, depending on which variety you choose.

The snowdrops are one of the earliest bulbs to flower, starting in January; some varieties will also continue flowering in succession for two months or so.

Freesias carry a spray of flowers on an arching 30-cm (12-in) stem, and they come in practically all colours; deep yellow or orange are the most common and have the most fragrant flowers, but purple, magenta, blue, red, white and rosy pink are also available. Flowering starts just after (or at) Christmas, and continues intermittently until late March, and their fragrance will invade the whole house.

Iris reticulata is a miniature iris whose flower stems grow to about 15 cm (6 in), though the leaves will be considerably longer indoors. It is purple and slightly scented, but there are varieties in various shades of blue and reddish purple. Flowering can be in late January or early February. (See also 'Fragrant Plants'.)

The grape hyacinths, *Muscari azureum*, mostly grow to about 15 cm (6 in) and appear in February, March or April; the blues are their colour, and one navy blue variety is quite distinctive. Most are scented.

The small-flowered daffodils are particularly charming; there are a lot of different species with variations on the typical daffodil-flower shape, and in all shades of yellow, gold, cream, white, orange and near red. A collection of all these different kinds is fun to grow in bowls; they are between 15 and 30 cm (6 and 12 in) at most in height, and flowering is from February until April. The Hoop Petticoat Daffodil, the cyclamen-flowered type, the creamy white flowers of the Angel's Tears, and the narrow frilly trumpets of February Gold are especially delightful. Fragrance is also part of the make-up of some of these small bulbs. (See also 'Forced Winter Bulbs'.)

The scillas, or squills, flower in February and March; they are tiny, 7.5–15 cm (3–6 in) tall, with wide-open bell-shaped flowers, blue or white.

The time to plant the majority (freesias are treated separately below) of these small bulbs is from the beginning of September to early October, depending on whether they flower earlier or later; the iris can be planted from mid- to late August, though early September will not delay it too much. Plant all these bulbs about 2.5 cm (1 in) deep, in other words, with that depth of compost above the bulb, in John Innes Potting Compost No. 1 (see page 8), not forgetting to put broken pieces of clay pot or other drainage material at the bottom of the container. As the bulbs are small, they will do best in pans rather than pots, planted about 2.5 cm (1 in) apart.

Give them a good watering, allowing superfluous water to drain off, and then put most of them in a cool dark place, such as a garage or cellar, or plunge them in a north border in the garden, covered with about 10-cm (4-in) depth of soil, ashes or peat. The amount of time you should leave them in the dark varies: the grape hyacinth makes its growth very early in autumn, and then stands still—it should only be kept in the dark for about a month —and the iris and snowdrops need not be darkened at all. Chionodoxas and scillas should be brought into the light in November, crocus plunged for about five weeks, and narcissus for six to eight weeks.

Once the period in the dark is over, bring the bulbs into gentle light, but leave them either outdoors or in an unheated or barely heated room until about a fortnight or so before their normal flowering time, when a little warmth of about 10–13°C (50–55°F) will bring them quickly into flower. Water moderately while they are growing or flowering, and feed with a potash-high fertilizer when the flowers have died down until the leaves begin to yellow. Then gradually stop watering and either leave the bulbs in the pans until planting time the following autumn, or remove them from the compost, clean them, discarding the offsets if they are not wanted for increase, and store them in a cool dark place. The iris is an exception here; it needs warmth during the summer to ripen completely.

The freesia, a native of South Africa, is slightly different in its habit of growth, and consequently needs slightly different treatment. The corms should be planted in early to late August. They need a good depth of compost, as they make long roots, and should have at least 17 cm (7 in) depth of John Innes Potting Compost No. 2 (see page 8). Plant them with the tops of the corms about 2.5 cm (1 in) below the surface, putting about ten in a 20-cm (8-in) pot. Water them in, and put the pot either in a cool shady position in the garden or indoors on a windowsill. Coolness at this stage is important; at the end of September they should be brought in and kept at about 10–13°C (50–55°F), though 16°C (60°F) will not hurt, in as good a light as possible. By this time they will need supporting, with split canes round the edge of the pot and string threaded from them amongst the leaves and stems in two or three layers. Water moderately and when the buds start to emerge, begin to give a weak feed about once a week and raise the temperature to about 16–18°C (60–65°F). Continue to water and feed the bulbs when the flowers have finished, dry off gradually as the leaves wither, and then remove the corms; retain the largest corms, clean them and leave them in as hot a place as possible until planting time so that they can finish ripening. The largest of the cormlets can be used for increase, and will flower in about two or three years.

Forced winter bulbs

Hyacinths＊, narcissi＊ and daffodils＊

Plants which flower at Christmas and during winter are rare in cool temperate climates, but it is possible to encourage some bulbs to flower then instead of in spring, partly by manipulating the amount of light they receive, and partly by giving them cool conditions much earlier than they would normally receive them. This latter technique needs to be carried out very carefully, and it is usually only possible for the commercial grower. Pre-cooling flowering bulbs ensures that they will flower at Christmas, and hyacinths, some of the narcissi and some of the tulips can all be treated to flower over the festive season.

Besides the Dutch hyacinths, with their massive spikes of closely packed flowers, there are the Roman hyacinths, more delicate in form with the individual flowers spaced much more widely apart on the stem. These are the earliest to flower, and even without pre-cooling they can be in bloom at Christmas. The variation in colour is not as great as with the Dutch kinds, being mostly white, pink or blue, but they are fragrant, easier to flower and less expensive.

Prepared Dutch hyacinths should be potted at the end of August; the bulbs are large and will need a pot at least 12.5 cm (5 in) in diameter, otherwise the roots will be so short of room that they tend to go round and round the pot and come to the surface. They will also do this if the compost on which the base of the bulb sits is too firm; leave it fairly loose so that they can penetrate it easily.

If you want to grow the bulbs again, use John Innes Potting Compost No. 2 (see page 8), otherwise you can put them in bulb fibre which contains fibrous peat, crushed charcoal and oyster-shell in the proportions by volume of 6, 1 and 2; this contains no food, so the bulb cannot develop a flower embryo for the following year, and will be useless. Plant the bulbs so that the necks are well clear of the surface, and put the pots in the dark in a cool place, such as a cellar or garage, covering them with black plastic, if necessary, to keep the light out completely. They should be left there for at least two months, but don't forget to look at them occasionally to see if they need watering. They can also be put out of doors, plunged 15 cm (6 in) below the soil surface in a cool north-facing bed.

Wherever you put them, don't bring the bulbs indoors until the shoots are 2.5–5 cm (1–2 in) long, and then put them in a cool—7°C (45°F)—shaded place until the flower buds have emerged completely from the necks of the bulbs. Only then can you give them more light and warmth; if too much warmth and light are given too soon, the leaves may become very long, and the flowers stop growing or not appear at all. Remember to water the bulbs all the time they are growing and support the flower stems; when the flowers have gone over, feed the bulbs once a week until the leaves start to yellow. Then gradually dry the bulbs off and store them in a cool shady place until it is time to plant them again. Do not try to force them in the year immediately following; grow them in pots at a normal pace, or plant outdoors.

Bulbs which have not been prepared can be planted in September or early October and treated in the same way, for flowering in January and February; by planting in succession and using early or late varieties, you can have hyacinths in flower indoors continuously until late February. Roman hyacinths should be potted in late September, and will naturally flower at or before Christmas without being 'prepared'.

Some good varieties for forcing are John Bos, rose, beginning of January; Delft Blue and Pink Pearl, mid-January; L'Innocence, white, and Distinction, burgundy, end January; City of Haarlem, pale yellow, early February (the months refer to the time at which the plants should first be brought indoors). Specialist bulb catalogues will indicate the best time to start forcing each variety, and its flowering time.

You can also grow hyacinths in water in special hyacinth glasses, but the bulbs will have to be thrown away afterwards; they cannot be grown again. All that you need do is put the bulb in the top part of the glass, fill the lower part with water so that it is just below the bulb base, and put the container in a dark cool place. Top the water up occasionally, but be careful not to let it come up high enough to actually touch the bulb or it will rot. The roots will grow down into the water, and look quite attractive in themselves. When the shoots have grown a little, bring the bulb and glass into the light and treat in the usual way.

As with hyacinths, narcissi—which include daffodils—can be obtained 'prepared' for Christmas flowering, or can be forced to flower a little later. The earliest bulbs can be potted in August or September, using John Innes Potting Compost No. 1 (see page 8); keep the necks well clear of the compost, and plant three or four to a 10-cm (4-in) container. Put them in a cool dark place for about six to eight weeks, and then treat in the same way as hyacinths. If you give too much warmth too early, you can damage or destroy the flower or produce plants with very elongated leaves. The secret is gentle forcing. Be careful, too, that the bulbs do not run short of water at any time; alternations of wet and dry compost result in damaged flowers or brown florets.

Paperwhite narcissi have fragrant white flowers with pale orange centres, in clusters; this variety can be treated slightly differently, as the bulbs can be put in a good light as soon as they are planted, but no warmer than 10°C (50°F). Cragford is white with deep orange centres, and Soleil d'Or is fragrant and deep yellow, with an orange cup. These will both flower at Christmas, though Cragford will need to have been prepared.

You can also grow these narcissi on pebbles in shallow bowls without any compost but, like hyacinths grown in glasses, they will be no good afterwards. Use shallow rectangular or round containers, without drainage holes, and fill them with clean pebbles to within 5 cm (2 in) of the rim. Put the bulbs upright on the pebbles, fill in between them with more pebbles and add rainwater to just below the base of the bulbs, renewing it as necessary. A little charcoal will keep the water clean.

Put the containers in a cool dark place (except Paperwhite, see above)—7°C (45°F)—until the end of November, then give more light and a temperature of 10–13°C (50–55°F). If you keep them on the cool side, the flowers will last longer. Ordinary daffodils and other narcissi can be forced gently, if you observe the basic principle of allowing them plenty of time to make root growth, followed by gentle introduction to light and warmth. Successional flowering can be obtained by varying the planting time and by using different varieties.

The perfume and colour of hyacinths are especially welcome in the dark winter months

Cacti

Aporocactus flagelliformis (Rat's-tail Cactus)∗ , *Cephalocereus senilis* (Old Man Cactus)∗ , *Chamaecereus sylvestrii*∗ , *Echinocactus grusonii* (Golden Barrel Cactus)∗ , Mammillaria spp.∗ , Opuntia (Prickly Pear)∗

You either love cacti or hate them; there seem to be no two ways about it. Or you may be in the first stages of becoming fascinated by their bizarre shapes and their ability to sprout flowers from the most unlikely places. Cacti are the Martians of the plant world; they are the only plants which can survive living in extreme conditions of heat and drought. Because of this they have altered their way of life and form so completely that they no longer look or grow in the same way as conventional plants.

Many cacti have developed a plant body which is almost completely round; such a shape combines the least surface area—and therefore loses least moisture by transpiration—with the greatest internal area for retention of moisture. Cacti tissue has also developed so that it is capable of storing water for extremely long periods, even during great heat. Many cacti are also exceedingly prickly or spiny, a development which protects them from grazing animals. Their roots are often very fine and close to the surface, but extremely wide-reaching, so that when rain does come they can absorb as much as possible for the short time it lasts; this root development is also essential in places where there are heavy dews. They flower mostly in May and June, but very briefly because of the short time during which moisture is usually available.

Cacti are, with the exception of the *Rhipsalis*, natives of North and South America. Civilization has, however, carried them to the Old World, where some, for example, opuntias, are now indigenous to desert regions there. They have a considerable fascination which is entirely their own: their figures, prickliness (or hairiness) and exotic flowers are all endearing and, moreover, they are not difficult to grow.

All the cacti described here are easy to manage, though quite different in appearance to one another. The Rat's-tail Cactus, as one would expect, produces slender, rounded hanging stems with a thick growth of spines and magenta-coloured flowers in early spring, each of which lasts for several days. The Old Man Cactus is so named for the mass of white hairs, 12 cm (5 in) or so long, produced all over it. It comes from Mexico where it can grow to 12 m (40 ft) tall, but it is very slow-growing and will not flower until it is about 6 m (20 ft) tall.

Chamaecereus sylvestrii is often seen growing in pots on windowsills and is embarrassingly easy to cultivate; it produces prostrate sideshoots with ease and rapidity, and each of these can be removed and rooted with equal facility. It flowers profusely in May and June, producing bright red blooms.

The Golden Barrel Cactus, *Echinocactus grusonii*, is chiefly famous for its golden spines, the tuft of golden wool on top and deep yellow flowers. It is almost completely round and is found in the deserts of central Mexico. It is also slow-growing, and in cultivation rarely reaches a size at which it will flower.

Mammillarias are sometimes called Pincushion Cacti. They are often almost completely circular and covered in bristles, with small bright yellow, red, pink or white flowers peering through the bristles in a circle round the top of the plant. They last for several weeks and are often produced in intermittent bursts throughout the summer, followed by red berries which may last through the winter to the new flowering season.

The Prickly Pear (Opuntia) is the one most people start a cactus collection with; it is practically indestructible and grows new 'ears' almost overnight. But it rarely does more than this, and after a season or two of watching it rapidly outgrowing its space, it can be tactfully given away to an unsuspecting novice! You will at least have learnt the elements of cactus management from caring for it.

The compost required for cacti is rather different to the usual John Innes potting composts (see page 8). They need very good drainage and you can use John Innes No. 1 with a sixth part of coarse sand added. Some of the coarse sand proportion can contain broken brick. Alternatively you can use a mix of 3 parts John Innes compost to 1 part fine grit, or a mix of 2 parts loam, 1 part peat and 1 part coarse sand (all parts by volume). If you use the second mix about 112 g (4 oz) of a general compound fertilizer should be added to each bushel, or alternatively a sprinkling to each 7.5 cm (3 in) potful. At the bottom of each container there should be the usual pieces of broken clay pot, brick or polystyrene.

Cacti like as much light and sun as possible at all times, and are ideal for windowsills facing south; they will take any amount of heat. In winter the temperature should not drop below 4°C (40°F); if you can keep it at 7°C (45°F), that is better still. Dry atmospheres do not cause any trouble, so you need not spray or supply humidity.

Although cacti come from drought-ridden areas, this does not mean to say that they will survive, grow or flower without any water at all. In spring and summer, they need watering almost as much as ordinary plants, giving them a lot when you do water and then leaving them severely alone until the compost surface is once more dry. In hot weather this may mean watering every two or three days.

As autumn comes, you will find that the compost is not drying out anything like as quickly, and you will not need to water very often at all. In winter—the cactus resting time—once a month will be sufficient, even less, especially if the temperature drops. Some people do not water at all between November and early March, but if the plants are kept in central heating they will probably need water every two weeks or so.

As well as water, cacti need food, like other plants, so the compost should always contain some to start with, and liquid feeding can be given in the growing season. A potash-high fertilizer, such as one of the tomato or rose fertilizers, should be given once a fortnight. This will encourage flowering, and prevent the plants from becoming too fleshy. When cacti do flower, the blooms are brilliant and exotic, and, contrary to myth, they by no means flower at night once every seven years! Instead they often flower every year for several weeks continuously.

Brown, red or yellow spots on cacti usually mean cold or wrong watering; a reddish tinge on young cacti means that they have had too much hot sun. Shrivelling shows lack of water and rotting at the base indicates too much water in winter. Mealy bug or root aphis are the main pests; see under 'Succulents' for treatment.

See also 'Christmas and Easter Cactus' and 'Epiphyllums'.

Mammillaria are cacti which flower profusely and easily from early summer onwards

Succulents

Agave americana (Century Plant)✳ , *Aloe arborescens*✳ ,
A. variegata (Partridge-breasted Aloe)✳ , *Crassula falcata*✳ ,
C. lactea✳ , *Echeveria gibbiflora metallica*✳ , *E. fulgens*✳ ,
E. shaviana✳ , *Euphorbia splendens* (Crown of Thorns)✳ ,
Kalanchoe blossfeldiana✳ , *Sempervivum arachnoideum*
(Cobweb Houseleek)✳

Although cacti are succulent plants, not all succulent plants are
cacti. In fact, there are a great many which are not cacti. The
main distinction between them is the 'areoles' on cacti which are
a sort of woolly bud carrying spines, hairs or bristles, and sometimes also flowers. In addition, what are commonly called succulents carry leaves or leaf-like structures which are only found in
two or three of the cacti. These leaves are usually very fleshy and
it is this part of the plant which stores the water, whereas in
cacti water is stored in the main stem.

Like cacti, succulents are common to areas of extremely low
rainfall, though they do not necessarily grow where it is extremely
hot and where they are exposed to a great deal of sun. Many
come from South Africa, as well as from South America. Whereas cacti are mostly found in deserts, a good many of the succulents come from dry prairie-like regions.

Succulents do not flower as prolifically as cacti, and may in fact
be regarded as foliage plants, as most of their beauty is in the
colouring and form of the leaves, often clustered in a rosette.
They do, of course, produce flowers, but rather small, or not
very many on one plant. Many grow straight out of cracks in
rocks, from between stones, or in soil which is mostly shingle
and where there is very little nutrient indeed. On the whole they
are slow-growing.

It is not surprising, therefore, that a very well-drained compost
is needed, probably even more so than for cacti. You can use a
cactus compost (see page 64) with an extra part of coarse sand or
grit added to it or stone chippings spread on the compost surface.
This is especially important in winter when the temperature
drops—cold and wet combined will quickly produce rotting.
Pieces of broken clay pot will be needed in the pot base.

When you water a succulent plant, give it sufficient to soak
right through the compost; the quantity will initially fill the
space between the pot rim and the compost surface, and you may
have to give a second watering before the extra liquid drains
through the drainage hole. Then leave the plant completely alone
until the compost surface is dry again; don't give it dribbles every
now and then because you're worried about it not having enough
water. Remember that succulents live for many months without
any rain at all, and can store moisture in their leaves to carry
them over such periods.

This treatment applies also to the plant's growing and flowering period; when it is resting, which is usually between October
and March, water it once a month if you are keeping it cool; if
you miss a month it will not hurt, but in warm conditions watering every two or three weeks may be required, depending on the
degree of heat. After the plant has been dormant all winter, it
may be difficult to get the compost thoroughly moist in the centre
of the pot. If so, a teaspoonful or so of detergent in a gallon of
water will help absorption, especially if the pot is put in a larger
container of water, so that the water rises about 5 cm (2 in) up

the side of the pot. When the compost surface looks damp, the
pot can be removed.

You need not worry about humidity in connection with these
plants, and the temperature in winter can drop to 4–7°C (40–
45°F). In summer most of them will not object to great heat or
sun, but there are exceptions which are not happy in intense sunlight, and these become tinted red or brown. Feeding will not be
necessary provided the right composts have been used; the
nutrient in these is quite sufficient for succulents, but it is advisable to repot completely at least every two years and, with some,
once a year. March or April, when growth is just beginning again,
is the most suitable time to repot many succulents, but if their
resting period is spring and early summer they should be left
until July or August. Some species flower between December
and February and then rest.

The Century Plant, *Agave americana*, was thought to live for a
hundred years before it flowered, after which it died, but in fact
it lives for a few years only. The spiny-edged, blue-green
leaves form rosettes eventually up to 90 cm (3 ft) long, and there
is a variety with yellow or white edges to the leaves. *Aloe variegata*
is also a rosette plant, with fat, V-shaped, dark green leaves
banded with white; if it flowers, it does so in winter, producing
red flowers. *A. arborescens* forms a cluster of several rosettes
which gradually lengthen; the leaves are spiny-edged, and
develop black spots if they get too much sun. It may also produce red flowers in summer.

Crassula falcata has grey-blue leaves arranged in layers up the
stem, and orange-red flowers in spring; *C. lactea* has smooth,
dark green leaves, and a cluster of starry white flowers in winter.
The echeverias are all good to grow; many are still called *Cotyledon*. *Echeveria gibbiflora metallica* is very handsome, with
rounded grey-green leaves flushed with purple-bronze spreading from a narrow red edge; red flowers may appear in spring.
E. fulgens forms tightly packed rosettes of spoon-shaped, grey-
green fleshy leaves, out of the centres of which come 15–30-cm
(6–12-in) stems with bright red flowers in early spring. *E.
shaviana* is a good new species with almost frilly blue-green
leaves, and pink flowers in winter.

Euphorbia splendens is the Crown of Thorns, with extremely
spiny fleshy branches, and bright red flowers dotted about the
stems in apparently no particular arrangement for most of the
year. It produces conventional light green rounded leaves, and
grows to about 90 cm (3 ft). It does not like cold and needs a
winter minimum temperature of 10°C (50°F). If the leaves suddenly turn yellow and fall, the plant is asking for a rest, of about
six weeks.

Kalanchoe blossfeldiana is grown for its clusters of bright scarlet
flowers in winter. The varieties Tom Thumb (red) and Tom
Thumb Golden are smaller bushy plants, remaining in flower
for several weeks. The Cobweb Houseleek is a rosette plant with
leaves crisscrossed by webbing and rosettes 2 cm (¾ in) wide;
pink flowers appear on the 7.5–10-cm (3–4-in) stems in summer.
It quickly and easily produces offsets and needs very little water.

As with cacti, mealy bug and root aphids are the main succulent
pests. Paint the former with methylated spirits; for the latter,
wash all the compost off the roots, repot in fresh moist compost
and water a few days later with resmethrin solution.

*Agave americana Variegata is a handsome succulent; the echeveria on
the right is also a succulent*

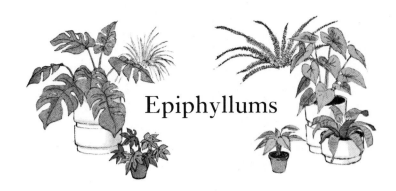

Epiphyllums

Orchid or Water-lily Cactus *

The beautiful flowers of these cacti and the fact that they are easy to grow are making them increasingly popular as indoor plants. Although they are truly cacti, they are a particular kind, rather different in form and cultural needs to the desert types. They are epiphytes, as are bromeliads and many of the orchids, that is, they 'perch' on supports well above ground, but they do not absorb food from their supports so they are not parasites. Instead, what little food they need is taken from leafmould, bird droppings and other rotting organic matter which collects in the course of time round their roots.

Epiphyllums are natives of the forests of South America, and also come from southern Mexico; they were introduced in the early part of the last century. *Epi* is the Greek for upon, and *phyllon* means leaf—the flowers are produced directly on the wide flattened stems, which look very much like leaves. Their old name, *Phyllocactus*, means leaf cactus.

Practically all the epiphyllums now grown are hybrids which have been produced as a result of crosses between *Nopalxochia phyllanthoides*, an epiphyte, *Heliocereus speciosus*, a terrestrial species, and various epiphyllum species—their ancestry might rightly be called mongrel. Since they have some terrestrial blood in them, they will grow in standard composts as well as mixtures which contain large quantities of leafmould or peat.

All this crossing has produced some extremely vigorous and floriferous plants; you can now expect your epiphyllums to flower twice a year, in May, and again in October. Each flower will last several days, and one plant may produce thirty flowers during one flowering period. The flowers are really quite breath-taking, at least 10 cm (4 in) wide and long, often larger, delicately but brightly coloured in various shades of pink and red, also yellow, cream, white, orange, salmon, magenta and cerise; some are fragrant.

The body of the plant consists of the flattened stems, perhaps 5 or 7.5 cm (2 or 3 in) wide, growing to a length of 1 m (39 in) or more, somewhat branching. It is rather ungainly and not very decorative out of flower, and it may need supporting, though some growers let the stems trail, with a little support underneath. Epiphyllums are shallow-rooting.

To make sure that your epiphyllums flower well and regularly, they will need plenty of light; a sunny windowsill is good, though midday sun in summer may be too hot. Remember that, although they grow high up in a tree in their native state, the sunlight is filtered to some extent.

The first flush of flowerbuds will start to appear in March or early April; they will be reddish and burst straight out of the side of a stem. By May they should be starting to open. You can try weak liquid feeding every three weeks or so during these three months, but it is not always necessary. Too much food will produce new stems rather than flowers, and the amount required partly depends on the richness of your compost.

Don't move the plant at this time as the buds grow to face the light and turning or moving it will make them drop. This may also happen even if the plant is not moved, if it is carrying a great number of flowers. It is simply Nature's way of getting rid of excess material.

Watering from March to May can gradually be increased until the plants are watered much as others are, and they should never be allowed to dry out. Rainwater is best, at room temperature. After flowering, take off some of the flowered stems, give much less water, but don't let them dry completely, and allow the plants to rest for a couple of weeks in a lower temperature; if you have a garden they can go outdoors temporarily in a slightly shaded place.

After the plants have rested, you can start watering normally again. New growths should gradually appear and, provided the light continues good, they will flower again in autumn. After the second flush of flowers, give little water between November and late February, just enough to keep the compost barely moist, and reduce the temperature to about 7°C (45°F), but still keep the plants in a good light.

Compost for epiphyllums can be John Innes Potting Compost No. 2 (see page 8), or a mixture of 6 parts loam, 2 of peat and 2 of coarse sand, together with John Innes Base (see page 8) at 112 g (4 oz) per bushel, or equal parts of loam, leafmould and coarse sand, plus the John Innes Base at the same rate. They are accommodating plants and will grow in a variety of composts, but they should not be put into too large pots. The root system is small, so 12.5-cm (5-in) pans or pots are quite suitable. You can also grow them in a trough on a window-ledge but, again, make sure the compost is well drained and crowd the plants in well.

Repotting will not be needed often, only when the plants become potbound, and it should then be done after the first flowering of the season. Epiphyllums are increased by cuttings, taking them off at a convenient joint from the top of a new shoot in June; leave the cut end to dry and callus over for about three days, and then place the cutting 1 cm ($\frac{1}{2}$ in) deep in moist coarse sand, supported by a cane. A plastic bag will encourage faster rooting, which is indicated when the cutting starts to elongate.

There are great quantities of hybrid epiphyllums available, but the following selection will give you a good range of colour and flower shapes which, although basically the same, have slight variations, from open funnel to flat, in the number of petals, the shape and the quantity of stamens, which themselves add to the flowers' beauty: Ackermanii, salmon-red with white stamens; Cooperi, white and lemon-yellow, funnel shape, fragrant, flowers from the base of the plant; Deutsche Kaiserin, pink; Eden, white and yellow, cup shape; London Glory, red; London Sunshine, mimosa yellow; Midnight, purple; Old Vienna, purple, orange and red; Professor Ebert, red; Sunburst, salmon and red; Truce, white with green back petals.

Some good species to grow are *E. anguliger*, greenish-yellow and white, fragrant, flowers 15 cm (6 in) long; *E. crenatum*, white, flowers 20 cm (8 in) wide; and *E. oxypetalum*, also white, fragrant, and opening at night.

See also 'Spring-Flowering Plants', 'Autumn-Flowering Plants', 'Cacti', 'Christmas and Easter Cactus'.

Epiphyllum hybrids are justifiably called the Orchid Cacti

Spring-flowering plants

Hydrangea *, Primula spp. *,
Sparmannia africana (House Lime, African Hemp)*

The hydrangea makes a very good flowering indoor plant for spring as a change from bulbs; it can be had in flower in March or April and will continue until June or early July. The hydrangea grown like this is the one with 'mopheads', large round heads of pink, white, blue or purple flowers. It was first introduced from Japan in 1790 as a shrub for the garden, though in cold or windy areas the flower buds are likely to be killed. Indoors, there should be no problem of this kind.

You will probably be given or buy your hydrangea in flower in early spring, and it should be given as good a light as possible (but not bright sunlight), and kept at about 16°C (60°F) so that it is reasonably warm, away from draughts. Give the leaves an overhead spraying every day, or kill two birds with one stone by standing it in water in a wide shallow dish so that the water comes up the sides of the container by about ½ cm (¼ in), thus ensuring that it is also continuously well supplied with water. Hydrangeas when flowering are very thirsty plants, and need copious supplies, so they will still need watering from the top with soft warm water.

After flowering has finished, cut out completely all the shoots that have had flowers; new shoots should already be coming up from the base of the plant to replace them. Don't worry if there are none, however; they will appear eventually. Prune away all but the four or five strongest, and put the plant in its pot outdoors in a sunny place. Replace the top inch or so of old compost with new, keep the plant well watered, and feed it fortnightly with a potash-high liquid fertilizer. In autumn the hydrangea can be brought back indoors, and encouraged to rest by giving it less and less water and keeping it cool—2–4°C (35–40°F) is not too cold. Leave it like this until the end of January, then gradually start watering normally, raise the temperature to 13–16°C (55–60°F) and give it as much light as possible.

If the plant begins to get rather large, you can take cuttings in August from the tips of new shoots. Plant two cuttings in a 7.5-cm (3-in) pot, under plastic, and then put them in the garden in a sheltered place when they have rooted. From then on treat them like the fully grown plants, except that in January when the temperature is raised they can be put into larger pots.

Pink or purple hydrangeas can be persuaded to turn blue by watering them with a solution of a proprietary colourant.

Primulas are quite different plants; they are herbaceous, not woody, and naturally flower in spring, though they are sometimes forced for winter flowering. *Primula obconica* has lilac, pink, white, red or magenta flowers, and rounded leaves; *P. sinensis* has fringed petals in a variety of similar colours; *P. malacoides* is lilac and rose, with a small, rather delicate, flower and frilly-edged leaves; and *P.* × *kewensis* has bright yellow fragrant flowers, and white-mealy leaves.

All primulas like cool conditions, though *sinensis* is a little less hardy than the other three and prefers a temperature of around 10–13°C (50–55°F) while it is flowering. Keep them all well lit, out of the sun, and water them plentifully; also feed every week while they are in flower to encourage a long season. Take off the

flowers when dead and remove yellowing or spotted leaves, usually the underneath ones. Watch for greenfly, too, which lurk in the centre of the plants and make the leaves curl.

After flowering, it is possible to keep the plants and flower them again the following winter and spring (all except for *P. malacoides*, which is an annual). Remove the remaining dead flowers and their stems, and repot the plants in new John Innes Potting Compost No. 2 (see page 8) in the same size pot; water them in, and then plunge the pots up to the rim in a shaded bed outdoors for the summer. Make sure the plants never run short of water and keep an eye open for red spider mite. Bring them indoors in the middle of October, again keeping them cool but well lit. You can start feeding them with a weak liquid feed when the first flowers are well open. Sometimes small plants are produced at the side of the parent plant, and these can be detached and potted separately at repotting time, using John Innes Potting Compost No. 1 (see page 8) and a 7.5-cm (3-in) pot; pot them on as they grow into a 12.5- or 15-cm (5- or 6-in) pot.

A word of warning about primulas; some people are allergic to them and their skin comes out in a rash after handling the plants, or even being near to them.

Another indoor plant which will flower in late spring is the House Lime, *Sparmannia africana*, a native of South Africa and introduced from there in 1790. It is named after a Swedish doctor who travelled with Captain Cook during his second voyage on a natural history survey of the South Seas and the Polar regions.

Sparmannia has large, softly hairy, heart-shaped leaves, and can grow up to several feet tall in the house; its fragrant flowers are white with bright yellow centres, and have their main flush in May. They will continue to flower spasmodically for most of the growing season. The plant grows quickly, but you can cut it back quite hard to keep it within its space without harming it.

The House Lime likes a good light and will be all right in autumn and winter sun, though hot sun in summer and sometimes the spring may damage it. Humidity is important, but mist it rather than spray it, and water it freely while it is growing. It prefers the temperature to be on the cool side; too high a temperature combined with dry air will make the leaves yellow. The minimum winter temperature should be 7°C (45°F) and the summer temperature 15–18°C (60–65°F).

When it comes to resting the plant, which is important if it is to flower, you can do one of two things. You can either stop watering the plant after it has flowered in May, when the leaves will drop. Then after four weeks cut the stems back hard to leave about a third of the length of the side shoots and half the main stems, or more if it is too big; repot in fresh compost (John Innes No. 2 (see page 8)) and start into growth again by watering heavily. Alternatively, you can let the plant flower on and off all summer, feeding it every three weeks or so with a high potash feed, and then gradually dry it off in late autumn, rest it until February in a cool temperature, cut it down and repot. If you follow this course, occasional cutting back of the sideshoots in summer will be necessary to keep it compact. Cuttings of new shoots will root in sandy compost, or even water, in warmth, during late spring and summer.

Gentle forcing will encourage the hydrangea to flower in late winter or early spring.

Summer-flowering plants

Hypocyrta strigillosa (Clog Plant)✻ , *Oliveranthus elegans*✻✻ , *Sinningia speciosa* (Gloxinia)✻✻✻ , *Spathiphyllum wallisii* (Peace Lily)✻✻✻

Although there is such a mass of bloom outdoors in the garden at this time of the year, it is rather nice to enlarge your flower arrangements by making up pot-et-fleur groups, an artful mixture of cut flowers and pot plants which are in flower, such as the ones described here. It may, of course, be that you have no garden at all, and in that case summer flowering pot plants will be more than welcome.

The Clog Plant, so called from the shape of its orange-red flowers, is a small shrub with shiny evergreen leaves, introduced from Brazil in 1846. At first it was thought to need quite high temperatures but, provided the temperature does not drop below 7–10°C (45–50°F) in winter, it will be quite happy. The flowers first appear in June and continue profusely to the end of July, on a plant which grows to about 17.5 cm (9 in) tall, but is quite a lot wider.

Water the Clog Plant quite freely in spring and summer, and give it a good light, but in winter it need only be kept just moist, particularly if the temperature drops; the fleshy leaves will help it to withstand lack of moisture at the roots. In winter it can be stood in the sun. Humidity is needed at all times.

Repot in spring, using John Innes Potting Compost No. 1 (see page 8), with a little extra coarse sand added, as hypocyrta likes good drainage. Give it a weak liquid feed at seven-day intervals from July until it begins to rest in autumn.

In the spring, just before it starts to grow again, prune the plant to keep it compact and improve its flowering. The flowers are produced on the new shoots, and cutting back the old flowered stems by a third to a half will encourage plenty of new growth. Increase can be either by division when you are repotting, or by cuttings taken after the plant has flowered, but the cuttings do need a high temperature of at least 21°C (70°F) in order to root.

Oliveranthus elegans has masqueraded under all sorts of names and you may see it being sold as *Cotyledon elegans*, *Echeveria elegans* or *E. harmsii*. It is a succulent plant (see 'Succulents'), but it looks more like a small leafy shrub than the thick fleshy-leaved plants of that group.

Oliveranthus, originally from Mexico, has leaves either clustered in rosettes or growing singly on the flowering stems. The tubular red and yellow flowers about 2.5 cm (1 in) long appear from early July to August. It can grow to 30–45 cm (12–18 in) tall, and in time may become rather sprawling. Give it normal summer temperatures, and plenty of light; water when the compost surface becomes dry and don't worry about humidity or feeding, which could make the growth too lush at the expense of the flowers.

In winter, keep the temperature at or above 7°C (45°F); water occasionally, and generally slow the plant down so that it has a rest. Start it into growth again in March with a higher temperature and more water, and repot in John Innes Potting Compost No. 1 (see page 8). Now is the time to cut it back a little if you wish. When new shoots appear, the 7.5 cm (3 in) tips can be used

for cuttings; put them in a very sandy compost, or even pure sand, and keep them moist and warm, at about 18–21°C (65–70°F). They should root after a few weeks, and each can then be potted, to flower the same season.

The gloxinia is an extremely mouth-watering flowering plant; its gorgeousness might almost be thought vulgar. The large flowers are open-bell-shaped, like a miniature trombone, velvety in texture and at least 10 cm (4 in) long and 5 cm (2 in) wide. There are many hybrids and colours, including brilliant red, pink, blue and white. There are also the tigrina forms, which are white, spotted and veined inside with the same colours as above, and almost more attractive than the single-coloured forms. The leaves of gloxinias are oval, velvety to the touch and dark green; the root is a tuber.

Gloxinia speciosa is a Brazilian plant, and it is from this that today's florist gloxinia is descended, via a good deal of hybridization with other species and varieties.

Watering must be done carefully, to avoid crown rotting, which results in the base of the stem turning black. When growth starts in spring, water the plant only moderately after the first potting and wait until it is growing quite fast before giving it much more. Always use water with the chill off it. Keep the plant in a good light, but never in direct sunlight, and supply a humid atmosphere; the shingle-in-a-dish method (see page 6) is best if you do not have a humidifier. Spraying the leaves is not generally advisable, because of their velvety nature, but an occasional misting over the plants in very hot weather will not hurt.

Gloxinias like warmth in summer, but after the flowers have finished watering and temperature should gradually be diminished. Keep the tuber quite dry through the winter, at a minimum temperature of 10°C (50°F), until potting time in February or March, depending on the degree of warmth you can give it.

Drainage of the compost is important, using either a mix of equal parts loam, peat and coarse sand, with half a teaspoonful of compound fertilizer to each 12.5-cm (5-in) potful, or John Innes Potting Compost No. 2 (see page 8) with a little extra sand. Put each tuber in a 10-, 12.5- or 15-cm (4-, 5- or 6-in) pot, planting it just below the surface. Give weekly feeds when the flower buds begin to appear.

The Peace Lily is a member of the Arum family, and so has the typical arum-shaped flower whose white petal is what is known botanically as a spathe. Spathiphyllum is evergreen, and comes from Colombia, so it does insist on a very humid and warm environment, with some shade; sunlight burns it. With care, it will flower twice a year, mainly in early summer, but again in autumn if you are lucky; it may even flower intermittently right through the summer until autumn.

Repot every year in fresh compost, and feed it through the growing season as it is rather greedy; it also needs plenty of water, except in winter from November through to March. The temperature then should be at least 13°C (55°F). Extra peat added to the compost is a good idea. You can increase it by dividing when you are repotting in spring.

See also 'Pelargoniums', 'Flowering Begonias', 'Plants to Grow from Seed'. 'All-year-round Flowering Plants', 'Climbing Flowering Plants'.

The gloxinia is a sumptuous plant with velvety leaves and flowers

Autumn-flowering plants

Hibiscus rosa-sinensis (Chinese Rose)***, Nerine spp. (Guernsey Lily)***

The hibiscus grown as a house plant is a shrub, originally from China but now grown all over the tropics for its beautiful and unusual flowers. The flower of this species is rose-red, about 12.5 cm (5 in) wide with stamens gathered together in a single column projecting from the centre of the trumpet-like flower. In Ceylon and other Asiatic countries, a red dye is obtained from the flowers and used for colouring food.

There are now many hybrids and varieties of the Chinese Rose, with single and double flowers, in pink, red, white and yellow, all very attractive. One variety, *cooperi*, has an added attraction as the glossy leaves are variegated with creamy white splashes and blotches, and their margins are edged with pink.

Hibiscus usually comes into flower indoors in late summer, sometimes earlier, and may continue through October. This is later than in its native country, because the light is less intense in more northern latitudes. The more light you can give it, especially when it is actually in bloom, the better it will flower, and it can even be put in full sun. The flowers only last about two days, but others take their place very quickly.

The hibiscus also insists on a humid atmosphere, and likes to be sprayed frequently, as well as needing water evaporating close to it. Summer temperatures can be above 21°C (70°F), provided there is plenty of humidity. In winter the temperature should not fall below 13°C (55°F), if possible; if the temperature does drop, it should only be for short periods and the plant should be kept on the dry side during this time.

Water hibiscus freely with tepid water in summer, and feed every three weeks or so from June onwards. In late February cut back last year's new shoots to about 5 cm (2 in), repot in a larger pot in John Innes Potting Compost No. 2 (see page 8), and begin to water, increasing the amount as the shoots develop. When flower buds start to appear, don't move the plant even to turn it round, and make quite sure the atmosphere is humid, otherwise the buds will drop off without opening. They will also drop if the plant is not receiving enough water at the roots. After flowering, encourage it to rest by giving much less water and less warmth. If you prefer, you can cut the flowered shoots back as soon as flowering seems to be tailing off but continue to water, and the plant will then very soon produce new shoots which will flower in their turn about two months later. But it is still a good idea to give the plant a chance to rest after this.

Cuttings 7.5 cm (3 in) long of the new shoots can be rooted, in compost or in water, but they do want warmth to do this, about 24°C (75°F). Watch for greenfly, which converge on the tips of the new shoots and stunt the growth.

The nerines are bulbous plants from South Africa which flower from late August to October. The flowers are rather spidery-petalled and ethereal, in delicate shades of pink, red, orange-red, salmon, crimson and white. They are easily grown from seed and hybridize freely, even germinating before they are off the plant, hence the variety of colours now available. Flowering bulbs can be obtained within three years, so that you can have the fun of producing perfectly good new hybrids without much difficulty; you might even produce some which are especially good and warrant registering under plant breeder's rights.

There are two main species, *N. bowdenii* and *N. sarniensis*, commonly called the Guernsey Lily though it is not a native of the Channel Islands. It is said that it acquired its name because a Dutch ship thought to have come from Japan was wrecked off the Channel Islands, and some of its cargo was washed ashore on to Guernsey. Amongst the cargo were some bulbs, which took root on the sandy beaches and went unnoticed until they flowered that autumn. However, no nerines grow wild in Japan, and it is much more likely that the Dutch ship had come from the South African Cape, where nerines had been discovered among the flora investigated by the Dutch. *Sarniense* is the old name for the Channel Islands.

The generic name of the plant also has a romantic origin. It comes from the name of the sea-nymph Nerine, one of the fifty daughters of Nereus, the wise old man of the seas in Greek mythology.

The flower stems grow to about 30–45 cm (1–1½ ft). In *N. bowdeni* (which is hardy and can also be grown out of doors) the leaves come in spring, and the flowers follow much later; after flowering, the old leaves die away and the plant should rest during winter, more or less dry and quite cool, about 4°C (40°F). *N. sarniensis*, the Guernsey Lily, flowers without leaves, which only appear when flowering has finished, continue until the resting period, and then die away completely in late spring.

Either kind, together with its varieties, should be planted so that only half the bulb is buried, *N. bowdenii* in spring, and *N. sarniensis* in mid-August. Plant one bulb in a 7.5–10 cm (3–4 in) pot, or three to five in a 12.5–15 cm (5–6 in) pot of John Innes Potting Compost No. 1 or No. 2 (see page 8) respectively. After watering them in heavily, leave them alone until signs of growth become evident, then begin to water normally. Keep them in a sunny place, but with only moderate warmth.

When flowering has finished, continue to water *N. sarniensis*; the temperature can be about 10°C (50°F). In May or early June, growth will cease; the leaves will yellow and wither, and it should be allowed to sleep. Thereafter it should be kept only just moist until it shows signs of life again. Put it in a warm place while it is resting, so that the bulbs ripen thoroughly, otherwise they will not flower.

Nerines can be left in the same pot for three or four years, and will flower better if undisturbed; the top 2 cm (¾ in) or so of compost can be replaced with fresh compost in spring or after flowering.

See also 'Epiphyllums' and 'Indoor Bulbs'.

Hibiscus rosa-sinensis, the Chinese Rose, is a shrubby plant from southern China

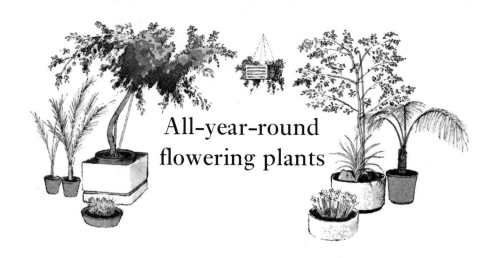

All-year-round flowering plants

Impatiens wallerana (Busy Lizzie)✻✻ , *Beloperone guttata*
(Shrimp Plant)✻ , *Abutilon striatum thompsonii* (Flowering Maple)✻

One of the few things Busy Lizzie and the Shrimp Plant have in
common is that they will flower all year, if allowed to. In appearance and cultivation they are completely different, though both
are extremely ornamental and mostly easy to grow. The one
difficulty is to get them to rest at some time during the year, but
if you can they will be much stronger and better-flowered plants.

How Busy Lizzie got its name no one seems to know, but the
generic name (*Impatiens*), impatient, refers to the sudden and
violent way in which the seeds are shot out when ripe. Tropical
East Africa is the home of the Busy Lizzie, so warmth in winter
and humidity all year are very important.

Pink, rose, white, red, orange and purple are the colours of the
flowers; a plant can be covered in them at the peak of its growth,
and a bushy well-fed specimen will flower profusely all through
the summer. There is also a variety with dark red leaves and
carmine red flowers called *I. w. petersiana*. The fleshy stems
show the need for copious watering—some of the family grow in
or close to rivers and lakes—and the plant will need watering
every day in summer. Humidity is vital, so stand it in a wide
shallow dish of water—it will not mind if its feet are in the water
occasionally—and spray overhead daily. This treatment will
ward off infestations of red spider mite.

Give Busy Lizzie a good light, but not bright summer sunlight
as this makes all the buds drop without opening. Winter sun will
not matter too much, as it is not very strong.

The temperature in winter should be about 7–10°C (45–50°F);
if you can keep it at about this from late December through to
late March, and water the plant much less, it should be possible
to induce a much-needed rest. With the spring, it can be encouraged to grow again by watering more and repotting.

You can make the plant bushy by pinching out the tips of the
stems when they have grown about three pairs of leaves; take the
stems back to the first pair, removing about 2.5–5 cm (1–2 in).

Use the John Innes potting composts (see page 8) and larger
pots each time you repot; by late summer the plant will probably
need a 13-cm (5-in) pot. In following seasons, older plants will
need liquid feeding in summer with a potash-high feed, but it is
usually better to take cuttings and start again. Tip cuttings or
short sideshoots about 7.5 cm (3 in) long will root quickly in jars
of water placed in warmth and a good light.

The Shrimp Plant has 'flowers' the same colour and roughly
the same shape as shrimps, anything from 2.5–7.5 cm (1–3 in)
long. The 'petals' which constitute the 'flowers' are actually
bracts, in most plants green, but sometimes coloured (bougain-
villea is another plant like this); the real flowers are white with

tiny purple spots, jutting out from between the overlapping
bracts. The variety Yellow Queen has yellow bracts.

Beloperone guttata was introduced in 1936 from Mexico, where
it grows to about 90 cm (3 ft) tall as a bushy evergreen shrub.
Although it is also evergreen as an indoor plant, it only grows to
about 30 cm (1 ft) in pots. Pinching out the shoot tips is not
needed as it produces sideshoots naturally and bushes out of its
own accord.

As with all indoor plants (except cacti), the Shrimp Plant is
happier in a moderately humid atmosphere; more water is
needed in summer than winter but it is not water-orientated like
Busy Lizzie, and if you give it too much it will soon tell you by
turning its leaves brownish-red. A good light, particularly sun,
will intensify the colour, so will lowering the temperature slightly
as it comes into flower. In winter the temperature should drop no
lower than 7°C (45°F).

John Innes Potting Compost No. 2 (see page 8) and a 13–15-cm
(5–6-in) final pot will be needed; thereafter you can topdress in
spring or liquid feed during summer. As winter comes try to
make the plant rest by giving it much less water and keeping it on
the cool side, just 'ticking over'. Don't worry if it loses some of its
leaves. In late February or early March, cut the shoots back by
about half their length, and use the tips of the new ones for cuttings if you want to increase it. They will root in compost, if you
can keep it warm.

The abutilon is sometimes called the Flowering Maple, from
the shape of its leaves, but actually it belongs to the Mallow
family, and the Latin name is taken from the Arabic word for
mallow. Several species can be grown outdoors in warm gardens,
including *A. striatum thompsonii*, but this species is probably
better with some protection, either in the home or a greenhouse.

Its heavily yellow-variegated leaves contrast nicely with the
dangling bell-shaped orange flowers, which will start to appear
in early summer and continue through the autumn and winter.

Abutilon is rather a twiggy, delicate plant, growing to a height
of at least 90 cm (3 ft), and very popular with greenfly, particularly if you do not give it enough water in summer.

Repot in spring every other season, using John Innes Potting
Compost No. 3 (see page 8) with a little extra drainage material
added. Give it plenty of light, except when the sun is very hot,
and a minimum winter temperature of 4–7°C (40–45°F). Feed
from late summer until the plant stops flowering of its own
accord in winter, then stop feeding and reduce watering to a
minimum so that it can rest.

When you are repotting in spring, you can cut back your
abutilon quite hard, by about half. If you take cuttings of the new
shoots and give them a temperature of 18°C (65°F), they will
root easily and may even flower by autumn.

The easily grown Shrimp Plant will flower almost all year

Throwaway plants

Chrysanthemum*, Cineraria*, Coleus (Flame Nettle)**

The chrysanthemum has been in cultivation for well over 2,000 years and *Chrysanthemum indicum*, with small yellow flowers, is native to Japan and China. Another species, *C. morifolium*, is white and yellow, and these two, amongst others, are thought to have been used for breeding during the course of several centuries, resulting in today's superb autumn-flowering plants.

The most recent development in chrysanthemum breeding was the production of all-the-year-round chrysanthemums, both as pot plants and as cut flowers. The normal height of the chrysanthemum is usually around 60, 90 or even 120 cm (2, 3 or 4 ft), but with the help of a dwarfing material which is added to the compost, plants can be encouraged to flower when only about 30 cm (1 ft) tall. The time of flowering depends largely on the amount of light the plants receive while they are growing, and the nurseryman can manipulate this to produce flowers at any time.

When you buy or receive a plant it should have one or two flowers open, and the rest in bud. If so, it will continue to flower for at least six weeks, perhaps two months or more, with the right care, and especially with fairly low temperatures. The chrysanthemum is a plant of cool autumn days, so keep it at about 10°C (50°F), give it plenty of light, and an unstuffy atmosphere. It will probably need watering every other day, and the occasional liquid feed will help it to keep flowering well without tailing off at the end. Watch for greenfly, which feed on the tiny leaves and buds at the tips of the shoots and are easy to miss, and leafminer which make wavy white lines on the leaves.

Bronze, red, yellow, pink, lilac, white and amber are all chrysanthemum colours; the flower shapes vary from the kind with outward-turning petals called reflex, to the incurves, with petals turned in to form a ball, and there are some which are somewhere between the two, resulting in rather a shaggy flower. The blooms on these pot chrysanthemums are nowhere near as large as the greenhouse kind, but what they lack in size they make up for in number.

Once flowering has finished, the plants are usually thrown away, but, if you are keen, they can be put in the ground outdoors; cut the stems down to about 5 cm (2 in) and, provided there is no danger from frost, they will produce new shoots, which will be much taller, flowering in autumn. Alternatively you can cut the plant down to an inch or so, keep it watered and when new shoots appear from the base, use them as cuttings about 7.5 cm (3 in) long. They will also be tall, and flower at the normal time.

Like the chrysanthemum, the florist's cineraria belongs to the daisy family, but the colours of its flowers are totally different. One kind is a particularly vivid royal blue, with a white 'eye' to each flower, and there are many other shades of blue, plus a range of colours like magenta, pink, wine, scarlet and purple. One of the good things about cinerarias is that they can be had in flower throughout the winter and spring, each plant lasting for about four to six weeks.

They are bushy plants, with large leaves, and drink a great deal of water when they are in flower. They are quite likely to want watering copiously every day—the soft leaves wilt very quickly, particularly in a sunny place. Cinerarias are shade plants, so they do best in a good light, but not sun, and cool conditions, 10°C (50°F). Give them much the same treatment as chrysanthemums, except that they need more water and humidity is more important. For some reason the cineraria is the caviare of the greenfly's world, so do keep a good lookout for them, especially in the growing tips and underneath the leaves. As cinerarias are grown from seed only, the plant will have to be discarded once it has flowered.

The third of this trio of throwaway plants is not grown for its flowers but for its leaves, which are brilliantly colourful and exotic. Unlike a good many of this type of foliage plant, coleus are not difficult to grow, provided you remember their great need for water.

The straightforward coleus have leaves rather like the common stinging nettle in shape, but a new strain has been evolved during the last ten years called the Fantasia coleus, with leaves which may be fringed, fern-like, fingered, curled like parsley or antlered, plus all sorts of intermediate stages of these forms. These extremely attractive shapes go with an equally attractive range of colours: emerald-green, yellow, bronze, flame, red, pink and magenta.

Some of the best, named varieties of coleus are Winter Sun, golden bronze; Buttermilk, creamy white, lemon yellow and light green; Crimson Ruffles, frilly deep red leaf, veined with lighter red and edged with bright green; Bizarre Croton, green and white leaves, splashed with red and brown; Dazzler, green, crimson, brown, pink and white; and Paisley Shawl, green-centred, with brown flecking and cream edges, flecked red. There are many more named kinds, but if you can grow your own from unnamed seed (quite easy with heat), you will have all kinds of variations, some better, some not so good, and all the fun of a surprise packet.

Coleus are bushy plants which grow all through the summer from late May until autumn; their leaves are at their brightest and most intense in a good light, but not in summer sun. The parent is a native of Java so, as you would imagine, they need damp air and freedom from draughts but, surprisingly, not great heat; temperatures between 16–30°C (60–85°F) are sufficient. Plenty of water is needed in the higher temperatures, but give less when it is cool and dull, and feed occasionally. If you put them in bright sunlight, the leaves will bleach. If you have a young plant, take out the tips of the shoots once or twice, to make it bush well.

You can keep the plants through the winter, but they must have a temperature of at least 16°C (60°F); even so the poor winter light will result in a pale-coloured plant, and they are rather unsatisfactory. It is better to use the plants for taking cuttings, keeping the parent plant 'ticking over' through the winter, with moderate amounts of water and as much light as possible. It will produce new shoots, from which cuttings can be taken in February; when they have rooted, pot them into John Innes Potting Compost No. 1 (see page 8) and 7.5-cm (3-in) pots and then, as they grow, into larger pots and richer compost. If you are growing from seed, it will need a temperature of 18–21 C (65–70 F) for germination.

See also *Primula malacoides*, under 'Spring-flowering Plants'.

Coleus blumei hybrids look best in full light

The fig family

Ficus benjamina (Java Willow)＊, *F. diversifolia* (Mistletoe Fig)＊＊, *F. elastica* (Rubber Plant) and vars.＊, *F. lyrata* (Banjo Fig)＊＊, *F. pumila* (Climbing Fig)＊, *F. radicans* Variegata＊

This genus covers a large and very interesting collection of trees and shrubs, most of which grow in the tropical or warmer parts of the world. It contains the tree which produces our dessert figs, *F. carica*, which grows wild in the Mediterranean region, and also the tree commonly called the Banyan, *F. benghalensis*, famed for the aerial roots which hang from the branches and root as soon as they touch the ground, producing a mass of separate independent trees. The plant so much grown as a house plant in modern homes, the Rubber Plant, *F. elastica decora*, also has the same method of spreading; it is the earliest known source of rubber and was used for erasers, the tree being 'tappable' after about twelve to fifteen years of growth. It is not used for rubber extraction now, however; a member of the Euphorbia family, *Hevea brasiliensis*, will supply rubber when it is five or six years old, and is widely grown commercially.

Quite a number of species of the fig family can be grown in the home without any great difficulty; they are all grown for their foliage and, as the illustration shows, the leaves of each are very varied in shape and size. *Ficus benjamina* can grow into a small, graceful, weeping tree, but it starts as a twiggy plant about 30 cm (1 ft) tall with narrow leaves between 5 and 10 cm (2 and 4 in) long. In its native habitat it is sometimes called the Java Willow, and in some tropical countries it is used as a street tree.

Ficus diversifolia, the Mistletoe Fig, is a native of India and Malaya; the botanic name means 'carrying different leaves', i.e. different to the other ficus species, but it is now, to be strictly accurate, called *F. deltoidea*. It tends to be upright rather than spreading, with small rounded leaves, in the joints of which the plant unexpectedly produces small yellow fruits—unexpected because it does not seem to have flowered. This is an old catch; figs do not produce flowers as such, but carry their reproductive organs inside a fruit-shaped container which later bears seeds.

The Banjo Fig, *F. lyrata*, is very handsome, but will need a lot of space to do it justice. The glossy leathery leaves are at least 17.5 cm (9 in) wide and 30 cm (1 ft) long, and are shaped just like a fiddle. It is a native of tropical West Africa and makes a good centrepiece for a collection of plants forming a jungle corner.

The Climbing or Creeping Fig, *F. pumila* (syn. *F. repens*), is evergreen, as indeed are all members of the fig family, and you can grow it as a climber, a trailer or creeping along the soil surface in a trough or box collection. The leaves are small but plentiful and the stems are aerial rooting; it is probably the hardiest of the genus, and will grow outdoors in sheltered gardens. What you must be careful of with this species is never to let it dry out; if the leaves wither, which they easily do, they are not replaced.

Ficus radicans Variegata is another creeping plant, rather irregularly variegated cream on the edges of or sometimes over the whole leaf. It is slow-growing but it can be trained up a support, or allowed to trail; either way it looks very attractive. It needs to be a little warmer than the other species, and always kept moist.

Ficus elastica decora, the Rubber Plant, is one of the first plants attempted by the beginner indoor plant-owner; it is not at all difficult to grow, and will survive a range of temperatures, light and humidity, but there is a great tendency for beginners to overwater it. If it is watered every day, after several weeks the lower leaves will begin to turn yellow and eventually drop. It need only be watered once or twice a week at the most in its growing season, when it is producing new leaves and extending its height comparatively rapidly, and in the winter in cool temperatures it can go for two weeks without needing to be watered. Make sure that the rootball is moist all the way through and then leave it severely alone, however much you are tempted to give just a few drops, until the surface is dry. This golden rule of watering pot plants is especially important with this plant.

There is a variegated-leaved form of *F. elastica* called Doescheri, which has leaves patched in dark green and grey-green, with creamy yellow edges. It is highly ornamental, but is slower-growing and needs slightly higher temperatures; too much water makes it brown at the leaf edges. A new and particularly handsome variety is Black Prince, with deep crimson, almost black, green leaves and a deep red growing point.

The Rubber Plant can be fairly easily increased by the technique known as air-layering, and it is a good way of shortening plants that are becoming a little overpowering. The time to do this is June or early July. About 30 cm (1 ft) from the tip of the plant, make a slanting cut up through the stem opposite a leaf join. The cut should not go right through the stem, only about halfway so as to form a tongue, which can then be kept open with a matchstick. Cut off the leaf on the other side and its stem, and wrap a handful of wet sphagnum moss round and in the cut. Round this in turn wrap a sheet of clear plastic to form a kind of sausage, and close it at each end with sticky tape. Put the plant in a warmer place, and after one to two months roots will appear in the moss. In autumn the top of the plant can be completely cut off with the roots, and potted separately. Dust the cut ends with charcoal or cigarette ash. Peat can be used instead of moss, but it is then advisable to attach the plastic sausage below the cut first, then fill it with peat and close the upper end.

All the ficus species grow best in a good light, though they are tolerant of shade; winter temperatures should not be less than 7–10°C (45–50°F). Keep them only moderately moist in winter and supply humidity, particularly for the small-leaved kinds. The large-leaved forms need sponging frequently with water to clean them. Repot in spring, and occasionally also during the growing season if they are growing particularly fast, but remember that the Rubber Plant will be happy in what seems too small a pot, a 12.5-cm (5-in) pot for a plant 60 cm (2 ft) tall, and 17 cm (7 in) for a 90 or 120 cm (3 or 4 ft) plant; it must be fed with a high-nitrogen fertilizer. Use John Innes Potting Compost No. 2 or 3 (see page 8). Watch for scale insects on all the species.

Ficus pumila Variegata (top), F. benjamina (left), F. Black Prince (right), F. radicans Variegata (bottom)

Fruiting plants

*Ardisia crispa**, *Capsicum annuum* (Christmas Pepper)**,
Nertera granadensis (syn. *N. depressa*) (Coral Bead Plant)*,
Solanum pseudocapsicum (Christmas Cherry)**

The fruits produced by the plants described in this section are not edible, except for the pepper, but they are very decorative and remain on the plant for a long time. They make an interesting change from flowers and three of them grow into bushy little plants, about 45–60 cm (1½–2 ft) tall. The Bead Plant is a prostrate species covering the compost with a mat of tiny leaves almost smothered in berries.

Ardisia crispa comes from the East Indies, where it grows as a shrub up to 120 cm (4 ft) tall. It was first introduced early in the last century for greenhouse cultivation, but will grow perfectly well in the house with plenty of humidity to prevent leaf drop, and a minimum temperature in winter of 10°C (50°F). It will not tolerate dry heat, so some method of supplying moisture in the atmosphere is essential, and you should also give overhead spraying, using tepid water; do not spray while the plant is in flower. It likes plenty of light, but not midday sun in summer.

Ardisia has white flowers in clusters in June and July, followed by bright red berries about the size of a small pea which last all through winter, and may still be there when the plant starts to flower in the following season. Keep it slightly on the dry side in winter, but water normally in summer; be careful while the fruit is swelling not to let the compost dry, otherwise the fruit will drop. Give a weak liquid feed when growth is well under way until the berries start to colour.

If the plant begins to grow too large, it can be cut back by about a third, and repotted into fresh John Innes potting compost (see page 8). Repot in March, and then water normally to encourage good growth of new shoots lower down the plant. When it has reached a height of about 60 cm (2 ft), it can start to lose its lowest leaves, and it is then a good idea to cut it back. Repotting may, of course, be needed before this.

Seed is the easiest way to increase ardisia, if you can give it a temperature of 24°C (75°F); use the seed from the ripest fruit and sow it in spring. Put the seedlings into 7.5-cm (3-in) pots when they are about 5 cm (2 in) tall, then give them the same treatment as the adult plants, and pot them on as they need it.

The Christmas Pepper has small red pointed fruits, very hot and pungent in flavour; the variety 'Red Chile' is edible, though very spicy. The word 'capsicum' comes from the Greek *kapto*, meaning to bite; the large sweet peppers and the hot chilli peppers belong to the same genus.

The Christmas Pepper's country of origin is not known as it has never been found in modern times growing in the wild, but it is on record as having been in cultivation since the middle of the sixteenth century. Unfortunately, at that time no note was made of who discovered it or where, though it is described in *Culpeper's Herbal*, published in the seventeenth century.

You can grow this capsicum from seed sown singly in March in a temperature of about 21°C (70°F), moving the young plants into suitably sized pots as they grow, and using proprietary composts. A final pot size of 15 cm (6 in) will be best for the adult plants; they can flower and fruit in these with the help of liquid feeding.

Whether you are given a Christmas Pepper or have grown it from seed, the treatment for the mature plants will be the same; plenty of light (with shade from the hottest midday sun), normal summer temperatures, plenty of water as they are thirsty plants, and regular overhead spraying. Spraying helps the flowers to set and keeps away red spider mite, which is very partial to peppers. Feeding with a potash-high fertilizer is needed from July until the end of September.

Flowering will start in June, and the fruits will form in succession and should remain on the plants into the winter, provided the temperature is allowed to drop gradually from autumn to about 10–13°C (50–55°F) in winter. If the fruit begins to fall, it may be due to dryness at the roots, dry air, too quick ripening, too much warmth or draughts.

The Coral Bead Plant or Fruiting Duckweed is a small creeping plant with tiny round leaves placed closely together so that they form a mat. The green and white flowers are equally small and unnoticeable, but they set to produce a mass of bright orange berries the size of peas, which virtually cover the plant, and last for several months.

Nertera granadensis (syn. *N. depressa*) is found growing wild in South America and Australasia; its name comes from the Greek *nerteros*, meaning anything lowly, and it was first introduced for greenhouse cultivation in 1868. It will, however, survive slight frosts and could be grown outdoors, though it makes a much better plant grown in a pot and given a little warmth in summer of 10–16°C (50–60°F); in winter the temperature can drop to 7°C (40°F) or less.

Nertera is shallow-rooting and therefore does best in a pan, rather than a full-sized pot; if you have not got a pan, you could half fill a pot with broken pieces of clay pot and then top it up with compost. The compost should be much more sandy than usual, so that it is well-drained. Although the plant likes a good deal of water, the leaves rot if they lie on compost which is always wet, hence the need for drainage. A good light is needed, also humidity, but not direct spraying of the leaves, and you should feed it with weak liquid fertilizer once every two weeks. Increase is by division in early spring.

Solanum pseudocapsicum, the Winter or Christmas Cherry, has berries which are pale green to start with and then turn yellow and finally bright red when ripe, so that in all their different stages of maturity they look very gay. The plants can be kept from year to year, and are usually available in the autumn. If kept comparatively cool from autumn until spring, at about 7–10°C (45–50°F), the berries will stay on the plants through the winter. A little occasional feeding and moderate watering at this time will be needed. When the fruits shrivel up in spring, the plant should be cut back hard, by about two-thirds, and given a little more water and warmth, and a good light. The new shoots can be pinched back once to make the plants bushier. As the flowers come, help them to set by spraying overhead daily, or put the plant in soil up to its rim in a sunny place in the garden, so that insects can pollinate the flowers. Make sure the plant doesn't dry out in hot weather. If the leaves or fruits drop during the winter, the plant is too warm, dry at the roots, or in a dry atmosphere.

See also 'Plants to Grow from Pips'.

The Christmas Pepper, Capsicum annuum, has bright red fruits from autumn into winter

Orchids

Odontoglossum∗∗ , Paphiopedilum (Cypripedium, Lady's Slipper)∗∗ , Pleione∗∗

A word of explanation about the form of orchids might make understanding their care and needs a little easier. A typical orchid, besides having a few rather fleshy roots (rhizomes), has a collection of bodies known as pseudobulbs forming the crown of the plant, and these should be potted so that they are just below the surface of the compost. They are not true bulbs, but a thickened part of the lower stem, and serve the same storage purpose as true bulbs. Once the food they contain has been used, they should be cut off, otherwise they rot. Orchids may be evergreen or die down at some stage in their seasonal cycle, and the flowers are distinguished from all others by having a 'column' of fused male and female organs in the centre of the flower, and also, usually, a 'lip' to the flower. This is most pronounced in the slipper orchids, forming the pouch at the front of the flower.

Orchids come from all over the world, mostly from tropical areas, but there are even a rare few in Arctic regions. Those which come from the tropics are, on the whole, epiphytes, that is, perchers on branches, in the forks of trees and so on. The cooler-climate kinds grow directly from the ground; they are what is known as 'terrestrial'. Orchids do not need standard composts or feeding, any more than the bromeliads, which are also perchers. Instead they should be given a compost mixture of 3 parts osmunda fibre, and 1 part sphagnum moss (parts by bulk), except for those orchids which require a good deal of moisture—they do better in a mixture of 2 parts fibre and 1 part sphagnum. Osmunda fibre is the chopped-up root of the Royal Fern, *Osmunda regalis*, and is ideal for orchids as it breaks down slowly and releases sufficient quantities of the right kind of food to maintain the plant over a long period.

The compost should be thoroughly mixed, moist and at room temperature when you are repotting, which is usually in March-April, or whenever growth starts again after the resting period. It is not necessary to repot every year. All the orchids mentioned can be grown in clay or plastic pots or pans, and it is important that they have plenty of drainage material in the bottom. Broken pieces of clay pot are best placed vertically, filling the container to a depth of a half to a third, depending on its depth.

When repotting, take away all the old compost from the plant —it will be soft and possibly unpleasant-smelling—and also remove any obviously dead roots and soft bulbs which are no longer green. Use the same size pot, and pot the orchid so that space is left at the front of the plant for new growth, of either pseudobulbs or roots. Put a little compost over the drainage material, and then work more compost in between the roots of the orchid and underneath it. Put the orchid in the pot and fill in more compost; keep the fibres of the compost running vertically, and firm it gently with a pointed stick. It is not necessary to ram down the compost, as it drives out all the air, vital to orchid roots.

You will have realized by now that orchid cultivation is an extremely specialized form of plant care. Orchids themselves have great variations in their type of growth and seasonal needs, as well as in flower form, but the ones described here are amongst the easiest to manage in the home.

Odontoglossums get their name from the Greek *odons*, tooth, and *glossa*, a tongue; the lip of the flower is said to be tooth-shaped. There are several flowers on one spike, large and very attractive, in a mass of different colours, produced in various seasons, depending on the species the plant is derived from. There are literally thousands of hybrids.

The standard orchid compost is suitable, and you should repot when required in spring or September. The temperature in summer can rise to 21°C (70°F) or more, though not much higher; in winter it can drop to 10–13°C (50–55°F); a steady temperature of 16°C (60°F) is ideal. Humidity is essential and these orchids should be watered, preferably with warm water, all year, giving less in the lower temperatures. Feeding is not necessary. You can increase them by dividing them at potting time, but make sure that each section has four pseudobulbs and one new bud.

The Slipper Orchids are so named from the pouch which forms the lip of the flower; the name *Paphiopedilum* comes from Paphos in Cyprus, where Venus is said to have arisen from the sea, and *pedilus*, the Latin for a sandal or slipper. The genus contains both epiphytic and terrestrial species, all of which are natives of the Far East; none have pseudobulbs. Flowering can be at various times in winter or summer, depending on whether the plant has plain leaves or mottled ones, and the flowers of some last for nearly three months. Flower colours tend to be in the green, purple, brown, yellowish-green and white range, with various combinations of these.

As they require more moisture than most, these orchids will do best in the compost mixture of 2 parts osmunda fibre and 1 part sphagnum moss. Repot in early spring as required. The temperature should be in the range of 10–13°C (50–55°F) in winter for *P. insigne* and its hybrids which are the easiest ones to start with. In summer they like to be shaded, fairly humid and warm, and should be freely watered with tepid rainwater. Draughts are bad, but they do need some air—a close muggy atmosphere is not good for healthy growth. Increase by division when repotting making sure that each section has three or four new growths.

The pleiones are almost hardy, and their time for resting is similar to those of the other two orchids described here. They come from India, and are sometimes known as the Himalayan or Indian crocus. They are quite small plants, only a few centimetres high, with relatively large flowers in various shades of pink, purple, magenta, rose and lilac; these are the colours of the outer petals, and the inner trumpet is often white, spotted dark inside, and frilly. The leaves die away in winter.

Pleiones flower in spring or winter, and need a slightly different compost, either equal parts of osmunda fibre, sphagnum moss and fibrous loam, or John Innes Potting Compost No. 1 (see page 8). Repot after flowering, putting the bulbs at 2.5 cm (1 in) intervals with the base on the compost surface. Water frequently in summer, once growth is well under way, and little in winter; feed the larger bulbs occasionally when they are in full growth with a diluted feed. Temperatures can drop to 7°C (45°F) in winter; in summer they should reach 21°C (70°F) or a little more. Moderate humidity is required.

Pleione formosana, an almost hardy orchid from Formosa and China

Christmas and Easter cactus

Schlumbergera × *buckleyi* (*S. bridgesii*, *Zygocactus truncatus*)✳✳ ,
Rhipsalidopsis gaertneri (*Schlumbergera gaertneri*)✳✳

The Christmas Cactus and the Easter Cactus are two of those plants which have suffered from the botanists' arguments and have had their names changed several times. The present state of play is that the Christmas-flowering one is *Schlumbergera* × *buckleyi*, and the one that flowers at Easter is *Rhipsalidopsis gaertneri* though it is argued by some that *Schlumbergera* is also valid for this one. They could well have changed again by the time this is published. However, both make up for their awkward and ugly names in their very attractive flowers, which are a little like fuchsias in shape and colouring, and last for several weeks.

The Christmas Cactus has magenta to rosy red tubular flowers, with two or three layers of petals, and a long cluster of stamens protruding from the tube. The first blooms appear in November and others open in succession, depending on variety, until February. The Easter Cactus produces great quantities of much shorter bright red flowers, rather feathery in appearance and less pendulous; its flowering time is April and May. The flower buds of both species are produced directly from the tips of the terminal fleshy pads which are the nearest the plants get to producing leaves. These chains of pads are, in fact, flattened stems, which have to some extent taken over the function of leaves. It seems unbelievable that these ungainly looking stems should push out a tiny bud, which suddenly bursts out into a glorious red flower, but the Christmas and Easter Cactus are two of the most effective of flowering indoor plants.

The Christmas Cactus is named after Frederick Schlumberger, a Belgian cactus enthusiast. The genus is found growing wild in the Brazilian jungles, though the hybrid was first recognized in cultivation in 1850. Both the Christmas and Easter Cactus are epiphytes, that is, they are plants which grow on other plants, but not as parasites; they are 'perchers', simply using, in this case, the forks of trees as supports. What food they get consists of rotting vegetation and bird droppings, and their roots exist in very little soil indeed, so when they are grown as an indoor plant compost is mainly needed to serve as an anchor.

To avoid confusion, it would be best to deal with each kind separately, otherwise the times of resting and flowering can easily get muddled. To take the Christmas Cactus first, flowering may start, depending on the variety, in November, December or January. While the plant is in full flower it should be watered just like an ordinary indoor plant, given a good light and a temperature round about 10–16°C (50–60°F). A humid atmosphere at this time is advisable to prevent bud and flower drop. Dropping may also occur if the plants are moved while in bud or flower, if the temperature is changed, if they are not given enough water, if the light is changed, or if they are in a draught or exposed to gas. In other words, don't alter their environment while they are in flower, and don't let them run short of moisture.

When flowering has finished, the plant will need to rest; give it very little water, only enough to keep the compost barely moist, but keep it in the same temperature and light. In May, or whenever the risk of frost is past, put the pot outdoors in a sheltered place, where it can be rained on, and raise it slightly off the ground on bricks. It will need a little shade, otherwise the stems go red. Keep an eye on the plant in dry periods and water if necessary, except in late August or September when a little dryness does no harm. From May to September the plant lengthens its stems and grows new pads, or produces new stems from the base.

In September, or before frosts start again, bring the plant into the house and give it a thorough watering; when the soil begins to dry out, water again and start to liquid feed every fortnight.

Flower buds will form and appear quickest during days which are shorter than the nights, and in temperatures on the cool side, that is, towards 10°C (50°F) rather than 16°C (60°F). If the plant is kept in a room where the lights are on in the evening, bud formation will be considerably delayed, but you may desire this to ensure that flowering occurs at Christmas or the New Year. Regulation of flowering in this way is best learnt by experience; the variety will also have an effect on the time of flowering.

Potting into larger pots and/or fresh compost need only be done every third year, in April, just as the plants are beginning to grow again; plants 45 cm (1½ ft) wide need a 12.5-cm (5-in) pot, and thereafter successively larger pots as the root system increases. A humus-rich compost is best, but well-drained; you could use a mixture of half leafmould or peat, made up with acid-reacting loam, coarse sand, and a sprinkling of bonemeal. The soilless composts are too lightweight to support these plants.

Although the Easter Cactus flowers in spring, its growing period is from June until late September, and it rests in late autumn and early winter. Flower buds will begin to push out in March. It is not as easy to get it to flower as the Christmas Cactus, but once it does start, it is much more free-flowering.

While the plant is in bloom, water and feed normally, then stand it outdoors in the same position as the Christmas Cactus and make sure it does not dry out. Bring it indoors before the cold nights start, gradually drop the temperature to 10–12°C (50–54°F) and water to keep the compost just moist. In late February the temperature can be raised to about 16–18°C (60–65°F), and watering increased to normal. Feeding may also start at this time.

Use the same compost as for the Christmas Cactus and repot, if needed, as soon as flowering has finished.

If the stem segments of either cactus become limp and shrivelled, the reason is usually dryness at the roots, but it can also be due to overwatering or a badly drained compost, both resulting in rotting of the base. Lack of flowering, as we have already seen, can be caused by too long a day or by too low a temperature from September onwards.

You can increase the plants by taking cuttings, using the end two or three segments of a new stem in spring or summer. Cut the stems off directly below the lowest segment and put the cuttings in the same compost as used for potting, with the lower half of the bottom segment in the compost. Three cuttings can be evenly spaced round a 7.5-cm (3-in) pot, facing outwards; it is best to allow the cuttings to dry off for two days before potting them, as this will help with rooting. Put a plastic bag over the cuttings, but air them every other day until they have rooted, then remove the bag for good.

See also 'Spring-flowering Plants', 'Cacti', 'Epiphyllums'.

Schlumbergera × *buckleyi, the Christmas Cactus*

Insectivorous plants

Cephalotus follicularis ✷✷ , *Darlingtonia californica* ✷✷ , *Dionaea muscipula* (Venus' Fly-trap) ✷✷ , *Drosera rotundifolia* (Sundew) ✷✷ , *Sarracenia purpurea* (Pitcher Plant) ✷✷

The group of plants which are called insectivorous, or carnivorous, are an interesting collection, because they obtain their nitrogen and other necessary foods from animal tissues, rather than from mineral and plant sources. Although they are primarily plants of tropical countries, there are some which are native to cool climates. Quite why some plants should have developed alone this particular, rather strange, byway of evolution is not clear; the majority seem to grow in very wet conditions, but then there are plenty of other marsh plants which exist on normal plant sources of food.

Plants are immobile, so the insectivorous ones have had to develop ways of getting insects to come to them and then trapping them. One group, the Venus' Fly-trap and the Butterworts, have developed leaves with exceedingly sensitive spines or bristles; a second group, the Pitcher Plants, have moderated their leaves or parts of their leaves to form really quite remarkable containers, complete with lids, which collect water and into which the unfortunate prey falls and drowns. The third group includes the Sundews, which secrete a thick sticky liquid—once insects are held by this, there is no escape. The stories one hears of fierce man-eating plants growing in jungles seem quite possible if this kind of plant can be grown in the home! However, the insectivorous plants that are grown in the home are quite tame, and you might well try using them instead of chemical insecticides.

Cephalotus follicularis is a pitcher plant, which grows in marshes in Australia. Its name comes from the Greek word *kephalotes*, headed, and is a reference to the female organs; follicles are a type of fruit. It is a small plant which only grows 5 or 7.5 cm (2 or 3 in) tall and forms a rosette made up of ordinary green leaves and also of dark green and light purple leaves which are modified to form pitchers. The lid has a netting of red-pink veins.

This plant must have a humid atmosphere, and it is best covered with a clear rigid plastic container of some kind—there are many frozen food containers available now which would be suitable. The plastic should be removed regularly for short periods so that the plant can obtain the insects it needs, unless you are prepared to hand-feed it. It needs a compost of living sphagnum moss and sandy peat on top of a good layer of drainage material, and it must never be without water. The temperature in summer should not be higher than 13°C (55°F), and not lower than 4°C (45°F) in winter.

Darlingtonia californica is another pitcher plant, named after the American botanist Dr Darlington. It was first introduced from California in 1861. There are two types of pitcher plants: those in which the pitchers are produced from the crown of the plant at ground level, and those which dangle in the air from quite high up on the plant. This species is one of the low-growing herbaceous kinds whose leaves are produced annually. The leaves can be as much as 75 cm (2½ ft) or as little as 7.5 cm (3 in) long, and arch up and over to form a kind of hood at the end of an inflated hollow tube. An unpleasantly tongue-like appendage

dangles from the mouth of the pitcher.

The main part of the pitcher is green, and the hood is mottled white and red-pink. Honey is secreted inside the pitcher to attract flies and other insects. Once inside they cannot escape, for the pitcher is lined with downward-pointing hairs, and they are then drowned and digested in the liquid contained in the lower part.

These plants like a cool shady place and considerable humidity: the pots can be stood in saucers of water, and additionally watered from the top. Repotting is best done every other year in early July, using a compost of living sphagnum moss, sandy peat and charcoal.

The Venus' Fly-trap is a native of California; Dionaea was one of the classical names of Venus. In this plant the insects are trapped by the leaves closing on them. Each leaf is edged with teeth, and there are bristles in the centre of the upper surface. When the bristles are touched, each half of the leaf folds upwards, the edge teeth interlocking, and the trapped insect is then digested at leisure. The leaves grow to 10–20 cm (4–8 in) long, and quite attractive white flowers are produced in July, on 15-cm (6-in)-long stems.

The usual compost of living sphagnum moss, peat and sand or charcoal is suitable. Give a temperature not less than 7°C (40°F) in winter and cool in summer, with plenty of humidity. The containers should be partly immersed in water, and the plants always watered freely. Repot in spring when required.

Drosera rotundifolia, the Sundew, is an English native plant, but now very rare; it grows in marshy situations. It is tiny, no more than about 10 cm (4 in) high with more or less round leaves covered in red hairs, from the ends of which comes a sticky liquid. Insects trapped by this are unable to escape, and the hairs will also curve inwards when touched to hold them captive.

The Sundew is quite hardy, and needs only cool conditions. Humidity and the usual compost are required, but the containers need not be stood in water, provided they are watered well (except in winter, when they only need moderate watering.

The sarracenias are evergreen pitcher plants, and *S. purpurea* is a native of the eastern United States. The pitchers are modified leaves, rather bulbous and erect, between 10 and 15 cm (4 and 6 in) long. There are spreading wings at the top of the pitcher and the lid which closes them is kidney-shaped. The pitchers are green and purple and the spring flowers are also purple, on 30-cm (12-in)-long stems, very attractive in their own right. Insects are attracted by a sugary substance produced inside the mouth of the pitchers, and are then trapped by downward-pointing hairs to fall into the liquid at the bottom of the pitcher.

This plant also likes cool conditions. Plenty of water is needed in summer, less in winter, and they need humidity and a good light, but not sun. Rainwater is advisable for watering. A compost of living sphagnum, peat and sand should be used, first filling the pot two-thirds full of drainage material then putting it in another larger pot with sphagnum packed into the space between the two. Repot in spring, but only if the fleshy roots are becoming crowded. Damaged and old pitchers should be removed when repotting.

The leaves of the Venus' Flytrap snap together to trap the flies on which it lives

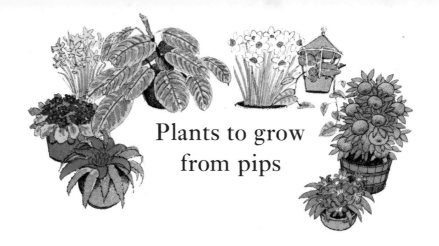

Plants to grow from pips

Citrus spp. (calamondin, lemon, orange trees)*, avocado*, date*, peach*, peanut**

A surprising number of the tropical fruits which are so easily bought from the greengrocer nowadays can be used to produce new plants without any extra cost. The pips and stones contained in them will nearly always germinate, and you should at least be able to grow an attractive foliage plant which may be evergreen, and may even flower and fruit in its turn. The pips from the citrus fruits germinate easily; fresh date stones will unfold miniature palm leaves; the big stone in the centre of avocado pears will sprout gigantically; apricot and peach stones, and the nuts from peanuts in shells, can all be sown and will produce seedlings.

Lemon, grapefruit and lime pips will grow into bushy plants with glossy evergreen leaves which, if rubbed, are pleasantly redolent of the flavour of their fruits; they have a strong possibility of fruiting. Oranges and tangerines, however, are not grown commercially on their own stock, and plants grown from their pips are therefore much less likely to flower, though you may be lucky.

To sow the pips, put them 2.5 cm (1 in) apart in a proprietary seed compost and cover them with their own depth. Keep them at 18–21°C (65–70°F). If they are sown in summer, germination will take about four weeks. When the seedlings have produced two seed leaves and one true leaf, pot each separately into a 5–7.5-cm (2–3-in) pot, using John Innes Potting Compost No. 1 (see page 8) with a little extra sand added. Don't worry if the little plants are slow to get away at first; they will take some time to establish while they are still small.

Pot the seedlings on into larger pots as they grow, and keep them in a sheltered sunny place outdoors until autumn. Pinch out the tip of the main shoot to encourage bushiness, and do the same with any sideshoots that appear. In winter, give them much less water and keep them free from frost. Flowering will start any time after about three years, in spring; spray the plants daily in the morning or hand pollinate if the flowers do not appear to be setting.

The calamondin (Citrus mitis), a miniature orange tree from the Philippines, is very popular and attractive with its fragrant white flowers and tiny oranges about 2.5–3 cm (1–1½ in) in diameter. They are edible, though rather sharp, and can be made into marmalade.

If you are given fruit from a friend's plant, the pips are likely to grow into plants which do not flower, but if you have the opportunity to take cuttings, the new plant from these will fruit within two seasons. They will, however, need quite a lot of warmth, 21–24°C (70–75°F), in order to root, and ideally the pots should be stood on a warm base.

The adult plants need a winter temperature of not less than 10°C (50°F), with a good light and good humidity. In summer, stand them outside in a sunny sheltered place. Flowers and fruit may be produced at the same time, from December through to the spring, and spraying the plants will help the flowers to set. After flowering, cut the plants back hard in April or early May.

With any of the citrus fruits, keep a constant watch for scale insect pests underneath the leaves and on the stems, and also red spider mite on the undersurface of the leaves; both are very partial to these plants. (See also 'Fruiting Plants'.)

The large conical stone of the avocado pear (Persea gratissima) is very gratifying to germinate. It may take months, sometimes only a few weeks, depending on how recently the fruit was harvested, before the stone splits in half and the surprisingly stout seedling stem comes up from between the two halves. Put the stone upright in an 8-cm (3½-in) pot of John Innes Potting Compost No. 1 (see page 8) to half its depth, with the rounded end downwards, and keep the compost moist. A temperature of 16°C (60°F) will give the quickest germination. The seedling will grow rapidly, and needs plenty of light to avoid becoming drawn. In its native tropical America, the avocado is evergreen and grows to about 18 m (60 ft) before it is mature enough to flower and fruit—it is not, by the way, at all related to the sweet pears eaten for dessert.

Pot the plant on as it grows to a final pot of about 30 cm (12 in), when it need only be topdressed with new compost. It should be kept free from frost in winter, fed weekly while growing and can be stood outside in summer. Humidity is necessary to prevent the leaves turning brown at the edges.

Dates, apricots and peach stones are easy to germinate, using John Innes or soilless seed compost (see page 8). Plant the stones about 2.5 cm (1 in) deep, cover the containers with black plastic and keep in a temperature of about 18–21°C (65–70°F) until germination. The date (Phoenix dactylifera) will produce small palm-like leaves about six or seven weeks later, if sown in winter, and grows into a nice little palm tree in two years or so; in the wild date palms eventually reach 30 m (100 ft) and only then do they fruit. Keep the plant free from frost and give it as much sun as possible; water freely in summer, and feed about once a fortnight. (See also 'Palms'.)

The peaches and apricots are unlikely to flower, but a few do, about seven years later, to produce fruit. John Innes Potting Compost No. 3 (see page 8), freedom from frost in winter, sun in summer, moderate watering and weekly feeding in summer will produce good deciduous foliage plants.

The kernels (nuts) from monkey nuts or groundnuts (Arachis hypogaea), can be used for propagation if you put them in potting compost (John Innes No. 1) any time between February and April. They should be sown 1.5 cm (¾ in) deep in a 15-cm (6-in) pot and given a temperature of at least 21°C (70°F); keep them covered with black plastic until they have germinated. After germination they should be kept at or above the same temperature, in the sun, with a moderate amount of watering. The plants will grow to about 30 cm (1 ft) and produce yellow flowers in summer. The flower stems lengthen and bend over when the flowers have set seed (the nut) so that the seedpod (the shell) is pushed into the soil, where the seeds ripen.

The avocado pear and the calamondin (Citrus mitis) can both be grown from pips

Self-propagating plants

Bryophyllum daigremontianum∗ , *Chlorophytum comosum* Vittatum (Spider Plant)∗ , *Saxifraga sarmentosa* (Mother of Thousands)∗ , *Tolmiea menziesii* (Pig-a-back Plant)∗

All these plants are good ones to start with, if you have not grown many plants before; they are easy to look after, and produce tiny copies of themselves from leaves or the ends of stems which can be detached and planted, and hey presto! there's a new plant. All four are foliage plants, and very decorative they are too.

The one with the tongue-twisting name, *Bryophyllum daigremontianum*, is a succulent; that is, it has fleshy leaves which will absorb a lot of water and retain it for a long time, because this kind of plant grows in places where there is a shortage of moisture, due either to the climate or the soil. The name *Bryophyllum* is made up from two Greek words, *bryos*, to sprout and *phyllon*, a leaf, and refers to the fact that plantlets grow all along the edges of the leaves from buds produced by the leaves.

If you look closely at these tiny plants, you will see that they each have one or two hair-like roots, so that if removed and put on to moist soil they will quickly establish and turn into new plants. They are not very firmly attached to the parent leaves, and in fact often fall off of their own accord on to the compost below and root in that. It is quite possible for one plant to produce hundreds of these plantlets in one season, so be warned— don't feel you have to grow every plantlet that appears!

This bryophyllum has arrow-shaped, blue-green leaves, with reddish-purple markings; the leaves can be quite large, up to 15 cm (6 in) long, and the plantlets grow between the teeth on the edges of the leaves. The tubular flowers are grey-green tinged with yellow and pink, growing in clusters at the top of the stem, and last a long time. They are produced in winter.

Bryophyllums come from Madagascar, and like a very well-drained compost (see page 8). In spring and summer they should be watered like ordinary indoor plants, but in late autumn and winter keep them nearly dry, and the temperature can drop to 10°C (50°F). In summer it can go to 24°C (75°F) or more. After the plant has flowered, cut the flowered stem back to the top leaves and repot; this will usually be in spring. Humidity is not essential for this plant, but it needs as much light as possible at all times.

The Spider Plant is extremely well-known; it is perhaps as much grown today as the aspidistra was by the Victorians. It has long, narrow, grass-like leaves, striped centrally with creamy-yellow, which spray out in a rosette straight up from the soil. The leaf colouring is most intense and contrasts best if the plant is kept in as good a light as possible, though not sunlight.

Its temperature needs are not crucial; 7°C (45°F) or even slightly lower in winter, and normal summer temperatures suit it. Some humidity is necessary, otherwise the leaf tips turn brown. In summer it needs plenty of water, but if you forget occasionally, it will not matter too much as the thick, almost tuberous roots can store moisture.

Chlorophytum grows fast, and soon fills the pot with these roots; it may need repotting two or three times in a season. If it gets too large, it can be divided. During early summer it will produce long slender stems, which have white flowers and/or plantlets on the ends. When the plantlets have grown one or two roots, they can be taken off and potted singly in 7.5-cm (3-in) pots, putting them in rather shallowly.

The Mother of Thousands, *Saxifraga sarmentosa*, has saxifrage-like flowers, white and yellow, which appear in a delicate, upright cluster about 15 cm (6 in) tall in summer and last several weeks. However, this plant is grown mainly for its leaves and the many trailing stems with plantlets along their length. If the stems are allowed to lie along the soil, the plantlets will root into it. The leaves are dark green, rounded and hairy, veined with white, the stems red. There is a very pretty variety called Tricolor, whose leaves are lighter green, with irregular white edges and pink to red flushing on the white, as well as red stems. The whole plant is more compact, and slow-growing; it needs a good light to retain its markings clearly.

The species is very nearly frostproof, so in winter the temperature can go down to 4°C (40°F) or even less, if it is kept on the dry side, but the variegated one is a little tender and needs more warmth in summer and winter, no less than 7–10°C (45–50°F) in winter. Both like humidity, and dislike summer sun; *sarmentosa* will grow in some shade. Both also need to be freely watered while they are growing. The John Innes potting composts (see page 8) can be used, but the plants are not heavy feeders and there is no need to use liquid fertilizers.

Increase is simply by detaching the plantlets when they are about 5 cm (2 in) or more wide and planting them singly in 7.5-cm (3-in) pots. It is a good idea, anyway, to take away a lot of the plantlets before they grow too large, otherwise the parent plant exhausts itself.

Tolmiea menziesii is also part of the Saxifrage family, and comes from north-west America. It was introduced in 1812 and named after Dr Tolmie, a Scottish doctor and fur trader at Hudson's Bay. It is quite hardy, and it is interesting to grow as a pot plant because of the way in which plantlets grow apparently straight out of the heart-shaped leaves; if you look closely, you will see that in fact they grow mainly from a bud produced at the point where the leaf stem joins the leaf, and the plantlet sits directly on top of the leaf, hence the common name, Pig-a-Back Plant. Like the other plants described, these plantlets can be removed and potted up. Small green flowers are produced in April, in a cluster on a stem about 30 cm (1 ft) tall. A little shade, and cool, moist conditions, both of compost and air, are needed, and it does like to be fed regularly, about once a fortnight, through the growing season. Repot in spring, in a proprietary compost.

Each of these plantlets from the Spider Plant, Chlorophytum Vittatum, can be used for increase

Plants to grow from seed

Cobaea scandens (Cup-and-saucer Vine)∗ , *Ipomoea tricolor* (syn. *I. rubro-caerulea*) (Morning Glory)∗∗ , *Thunbergia alata* (Black-eyed Susan)∗

These three plants which can be grown from seed are all climbing, flowering plants; they are not difficult to germinate and, although they are mostly grown in the house as one-season plants, the Cup-and-saucer Vine can in fact be kept in a greenhouse from year to year. As might be imagined, they grow quickly and flower profusely, provided, and this is important, they are given as much light as possible.

The Cup-and-saucer Vine attaches itself to its support by tendrils and in the wild grows to at least 6 m (20 ft), so you must allow it plenty of space and supports, though in the home it will probably not grow to even half this height. It starts to flower round about June and will continue right through to autumn; the long-stemmed flowers are the shape of Canterbury bells with a flat, pale green and violet ruff round the base, which is the 'saucer'. They open a pale greenish cream colour and turn purple as they mature, with a cluster of long curling stamens projecting out of the 'cup'.

Seed can be sown in February, edgeways on, in a temperature of 13–16°C (55–60°F), using a seed compost; cover the containers with black plastic until germination. If the seeds do not germinate, it is probably because they are old, and it is therefore important to try and obtain fresh seed for reliable germination. Give the seedlings plenty of light and keep them warm in a humid atmosphere; put them singly into 5- or 7.5-cm (2- or 3-in) pots, depending on the size of root. Sometimes you can buy the small plants, the nurseryman having done the work of propagation for you. But, whatever the source of supply, cobaea will need plenty of water while it is growing and flowering, and it should be potted on once or twice into larger pots and fresh compost (John Innes Potting Compost No. 2 (see page 8)). Light is very important, both for flower production, and for intensity of flower colour; the flowers tend to be rather wishy-washy in a poor light, and the growth is straggly.

Normal summer temperatures will suit them and a moderately humid atmosphere; towards the end of the summer, feeding with a potash-high fertilizer will keep the flowers going well.

Cobaea comes from Central and South America and was introduced in 1787. It is named after Father Cobo, a Spanish Jesuit and naturalist.

The Morning Glory has been subjected to so many name changes by the botanists, having been called at various times *Convolvulus*, *Ipomoea* and *Pharbitis*, with a number of different specific names to each, that I shall stick to its common name. The Latin name given in the heading seems to be the one under which it is best known botanically, but *I. coccinea* and *Pharbitis* are both currently quoted for it as well.

The typical Morning Glory has brilliant blue wide-open trumpet-shaped flowers, changing to pale purple as they die; they only last a day, but so many new ones are being produced all the time that it is continuously in flower. It is a twining annual plant, a native of the tropics, where it grows to 3m (10 ft). It needs plenty of warmth and a fertile soil. The Sweet Potato is a member of the same family.

The Morning Glory has quite large brown-black seeds about ½ cm (¼ in) long, which should be sown in March in a temperature of 18°C (65°F). If you make a small nick in them first with a knife, this will help them germinate more certainly and quickly. They dislike disturbance, so are best sown singly in small peat pots, putting them edgeways on and covering them with their own depth of seed compost. Sufficient warmth is most important; although they will germinate at a lower temperature, the seedling leaves gradually turn white and the seedling dies. You should also be careful not to put the seedlings or young plants in bright sunlight, as the same thing will happen. Too wet a seed compost results in rotting of the seed so make sure that it is moist when the seeds are sown, but don't water again until the seedlings appear, unless it becomes very dry. It shouldn't, with a plastic sheet over it.

Pot the seedlings on, complete with the peat pot, in successively larger pots up to about 20 cm (8 in) diameter, and pinch out the growing tip of the plant when it is about 10 or 12 cm (4 or 5 in).

During the whole of the season, warmth, humidity and a good light will produce strong-growing, profusely flowering plants. They will want plenty of water and, as with cobaea, liquid feeding towards the end of the season with a potash-high fertilizer. Provide plenty of support.

The third of this trio, Black-eyed Susan, is nowhere as rampant as the other two. It grows wild in South Africa, up to a height of about 1.8 m (6 ft); in a pot the height will be about 1.2 m (4 ft). Twining round its supports, thunbergia is a comparatively contained annual climber, coming into flower in May and continuing until October. The flowers are pale orange, with dark, black-brown centres, produced in large quantities. Instead of training the stems in a vertical direction, you can grow it as a trailer hanging on a wall; the hanging stems dotted with the orange flowers look very attractive, and make an unusual specimen.

Sow the seed in March or early April, in seed compost and a temperature of 18°C (65°F); you can prick the seedlings out when they have grown two seed leaves and the first true leaf, either singly into a 7.5-cm (3-in) pot or several into a small box; the plastic punnets that soft fruit is sold in are suitable for tiny plants. For flowering, transfer them to 12.5-cm (5-in) pots, using John Innes Potting Compost No. 2 (see page 8); give them temperatures of over 16°C (60°F). Humidity is important and as much light as possible, with the usual exception of bright summer sun, which can not only damage the leaves but will result in the colour of the flowers fading. Give them plenty of water, and feed occasionally from August onwards.

See also 'Flowering Climbing Plants'.

The Cup-and-saucer Vine, Cobaea scandens, which flowers all summer without a break

Index

The Publishers would like to thank the following individuals and organizations for their kind permission to reproduce the photographs in this book:

A-Z Botanical Collection: 23, 37;
Bernard Alfieri: 89;
Melvin Grey: 7, 15, 21, 25, 29, 31, 39, 43, 47, 51, 55, 57, 63, 81, 91 jacket front;
Leslie Johns: 33;
Giuseppe Mazza: 9, 11, 13, 17, 19, 27, 69, 77, 79, 89, endpapers and flaps;
G. E. Hyde: 35, 45, 53, 87, 95;
Harry Smith: 41, 49, 59 & back jacket, 61, 65, 67, 73, 75, 85, 93;
Bill McLaughlin: 71.

The line illustrations are by Barrington Barber.